REPRODUCTIONS
OF THE EMPTY FLAGPOLE

REPRODUCTIONS
OF THE EMPTY FLAGPOLE

Eileen R. Tabios

MARSH HAWK PRESS ❧ NEW YORK ❧ 2002

First Edition
02 03 7 6 5 4 3 2 1
Marsh Hawk Press books are published by Poetry Mailing List, Inc.,
a not-for-profit corporation under United States Internal Revenue Code.
Book Design: Sandy McIntosh
Cover Photo: "Rose and Thorn" by Cal Strobel
Printed in the United States by McNaughton & Gunn
Acknowledgements begin on page 122

Library of Congress Cataloging-in-Publication Data

Tabios, Eileen.
Reproductions of the empty flagpole / Eileen R. Tabios.— 1st ed.
p. cm.
ISBN 0-9713332-8-9
I. Title.
PS3570.A234 R46 2002
821'.914—dc21

2002008770

Marsh Hawk Press
PO Box 220, Stuyvesant Station,
New York, NY 10009
www.marshhawkpress.org

For
Leona Florentino (1849-1884)
Magdalena Jalandoni (1891-1978)
Angela Manalang Gloria (1907-1996)

TABLE OF CONTENTS

Don't take my word for this.
Put no head above your own.
Have your own experience.
— Buddha

Cling to the earth / in skyward trance
Cling to the earth / in skyward dance
—Jose "Joey" Ayala

MY GREECE

When a term like symmetria is used by a late antique rhetorician, one should probably not expect it to have the rigorous precision of meaning that it conveyed to a sculptor of the fifth century B.C. In general, it may be expected that the technical value of a particular term—that is, the value which is dependent upon the special knowledge and training of a particular group— will diminish as the size of the group using the term increases
—from "The Ancient View of Greek Art" by J.J. Pollitt

ECLIPSE

The map of places passes.
The reality of paper tears. . . .

Holes in maps look through to nowhere.
 — **Laura Riding Jackson**

And because I don't know what else to do, I flee to an alien land whose history has become like you—impossible to be grasped. To escape chaos, the Greeks created art with abstractions. It is a familiar approach, having long used geometry to deny myself caresses. Oh—but now to feel the white-haired woman I will become sitting by herself, looking through a window and seeing only snow. I know nothing after all. I have become the smile of the *kouros* with a critical difference: I symbolize nothing.

She knows she said I won't reach out to you again. But even as I write this, I don't think I'll have broken that promise. You don't exist. I never entered a dark building after the high heels you love tip-toed around potholes. I never rode an elevator whose walls presented cracks so I could feel the embrace of leers. I never walked down a hallway clouded by an air I was scared to breathe. I never entered a room where you raised your voice in anger at me. I never entered a room where you exist. I was never

      felled
         through a rip in space where I felt you sculpting a dispassionate embrace.

The shards of geometry are all that are left to me: I attempt the poem, only to repeat consistent failures. But I would like to keep trying as I fear the chaos you rightly said I've never experienced. I long have known that I wouldn't survive chaos. You have. What does this say about me? What does this say about you? Now, I struggle everyday to determine how I can continue writing when I have heard my Muse whisper how small I am.

She is in a panic. And when she sends this to you, I know she is reaching out to a void. You don't exist. I am falling. And you don't exist: so where have I been?

How does she know I will betray Lucretius?

And how has she become a shadow when there is no light . . .

THE KRITIOS BOY

— for Jerome Pollitt

But what does it mean for a warrior to fall in love with his victim the moment he plunges a sword? My mother says I am long overdue for "spawning progeny." It is true: I cannot recall the year I last received a bouquet of spring flowers, even the most modest nosegay of bluebells. But I do remember tiny petals unfurling around yellow hearts. Below a blanket of pollen, they were dotted with moles—like the artist's faint scratches to depict locked eyes between Achilles and the Amazon queen Penthesilea as his sword penetrated her breast.

I am unsure with metaphors—I allow them to bleed from my pen, only to feel the "new uneasiness" among the Greeks shortly after emerging victorious from the Persian Wars. I am compelled to nod when I see the marble "Kritios Boy" break the tradition of the *kouros* stance. By shifting away from a rigid, full frontal position, the right leg slightly bent, the statue seems immortalized in hesitation. Many centuries later, I look at a photograph of the "Kritios Boy" and feel my spine begin to curve. I would like to fall, I think as I peep at the faces of strangers surrounding me in the cafe. I would like to bite my knees to mimic a snake swallowing its tail. She aborts histrionics with a memory of welcoming that particular day with a promise to buy herself yellow roses. She had anticipated that during the hours of their blooming, she also would allow herself a memory of fiction: a lover offering her the dozen blooms after a soft kiss on her unlined brow, a toddler playing by her feet.

I look again at the "Kritios Boy" and am appalled. Children should never become symbols for the mysteries their parents can never solve. I learned this lesson when I was six years old and gave a poor neighbor an old dress. I still had treasured the white eyelet lace edging its hem and sleeves. But my neighbor's parents cut them off to approximate a dress never worn—a blue dress imprinted with yellow abstract flakes. I had called the yellows

15

"roses." My poor neighbor had called them "daffodils." I had preserved her illusion with a polite silence. But no consolation exists in a memory I now possess that never fails to make me catch my breath.

PURITY

Once, the Greeks tolerated subjection to obviate chaos. But an attitude of detachment is like anxiety—a flower in a glass prison. So "the entire male population of Miletus was put to the sword and the women and children were sent into Asia as slaves." I look up from the page into the dying days of the 21st century. I am feeling the inhumanly fast beating of a woman's heart as she raises a rifle, then shoots a canvas with pellets of paint. I am feeling a deer quicken its leaps. The artist avoided the aftermath of wounds, but I see red.

After the fall of Miletus, the poet Phrynichos staged a drama about it. But the play's performance was forbidden by Athenians who fined him "for reminding them of afflictions which affected them intimately." I consider my search for unrelenting intimacy— a search I conduct despite my heart's cocoon of encaustic. I consider how a grid is supposed to eliminate gesture from paint. Although paint, finally, must return to its nature and flow like a menstruation—ooze with a viscous intensity unmitigated by geometry.

Though the Greeks would come to thwart the Persian invasion, I believe it noteworthy that such a victory belied intention. The Greeks—like all of us, through all of time—first attempted compromise. Now, encaustic fails and my heart looks me in the eye. I am compelled to answer the many variations of the same question: Why do I weep before a square canvas depicting a square? Or a circular canvas depicting a circle? Have the Greeks attained purity? Attained perfection? Have I earned the moments I made my mother cry?

TO BE SEEN BY IAMOS, CALCHAS AND TEIRESIAS

An old seer "ponders everything, but is unable to find a way." An anonymous sculptor carves the old seer with his right hand tugging at his beard. The stone shrinks as the seer peruses a sabotaged chariot. With his powers of prophecy, the old seer foretells the chariot will collapse and kill the father who would prevent a daughter from marrying a man she loves. This story has reached me beyond its origin in Archaic Greece to surface a question: how far will I descend for love?

Long ago I betrayed all ancestors for an unrequited love. Once, I reached into a cage to pat a tiger. It was his nature: the animal drew blood. We locked gazes after his act, and I believe regret caused him to bank down the embers in his sunset eyes before backing away to the far wall of his cell. I wanted to offer my hand once more but knew the blood would make him shrink in dismay, like when I kept telling you, "You are not hurting me"—and each repetition only made you lash out until I was a fetal heap on the other side of your locked door.

There are so many layers to any story. How a daughter sacrificed a father for a stranger. How that daughter asked a man who loved her to replace the metal pins in the wheels of her father's chariot with wax. How the man performed the favor though he knew it would not prevent the woman he loved from marrying another. Hippodameia, the daughter; King Oinomaos, the father; Myrtilos, the saboteur; Pelops, with whom the daughter fell in love—your figures lack limbs today as you stand before strangers like me visiting the Temple of Zeus. Your statues manifest the tragedy that moves me, *moves me*. I see my future in your broken bodies—spaces between stones signifying this world's only certainty: *Uncertainty*.

Hippodameia freezes in a posture of raising her veil from her shoulders. Perhaps as a symbol of her role as bride, a scholar suggests, or simply in preparation for a journey? I look at Hippodameia today: feet broken off at the ankles, a crack extending from below her right eye towards her hairline, a missing left arm. I believe she is raising the veil to hide herself from me: the reflection she would wish not to exist because, in Archaic Greece, they feared chaos. Hippodameia has recognized me: a saboteur waiting to be caught. Yet again, I look behind my shoulder, surreptitiously.

ETHOS

She is missing the tip of her nose. Yet I think of sultry women in leopard coats, flashes of violet eyes and slanted cheekbones behind fur. She is missing her hands. Yet I feel her pulling me out of bed where I had burrowed into pillows fatted by goose down. She is missing most of her body below her waist. Yet she stiffens my spine so that I leave the bed we have never shared. I consider this photograph of Athena, 460 B.C. It seems her form barely affected the block of marble from which she was carved. Stolid stone—you refuse the ornaments of the Archaic period to display essence. Ancient marble—you reach across the years to contradict what the people of my age had considered a truism: an object can never manifest its Ideal.

Photograph of an ancient sculpture—how many dimensions may be defined before my sight touches its target? You evoke an old poem I wrote that made others scoff and label me a "mere girl." I thought to honor the lucidity of objects that manifest intention— like the feather, the diamond, the rose and others now fallen from the sieve my memory has fought against becoming. When people laughed at my poor poem, I bowed in shame and slunk away. Now, Athena wipes my tears and notes: the girl offered truth because the girl retained the innocence of youth.

Once, you hovered because, you said, you wished to know how long I can retain my *Idealism*.

RETURNING THE BORROWED TONGUE

The, hands, on, the, piano, are, armless,
—José Garcia Villa

In 1898, the United States claimed it owned the Philippines after buying it for $20 million dollars from Spain through the Treaty of Paris. The Filipinos—who had won and declared their independence from Spain—protested, and thus commenced the Philippine-American War, a war that has been called the United States' "First Vietnam." With their prowess on the military terrain, the United States defeated the Philippines. The United States solidified its colonial domination through the cultural and linguistic terrain with the popularization of English as the preferred language for education, administration, commerce and daily living. Thus, English is sometimes called by Filipinos to be "the borrowed tongue," though enforced tongue would be more accurate.

JADE

I can see how I've misinterpreted the fall of night. Against a Grecian urn, shadows sunder. The clay is ageless and I ache to press my forehead against it. Once, I stopped a burn on my fingertips by peeling a grape. I forced perfection on its nakedness.

It is so difficult to find innocence in accomplished men. There is always something to be paid. Once, someone asked for my views on fidelity. Upon confirming the questioner was not discussing radio waves, I nodded and proclaimed with gusto, "Sexual fidelity is an admirable trait. I believe all my lovers should possess it."

I never show my scars, though allow an occasional easing of pressure with a flushed countenance. My favorite stone is jade for the impassivity of its face. Perhaps I will meet an optical illusion that is solid. That would surprise me like a boulder sporting a black, bowler hat.

My friends are astounded at my naivete. I met a man attending a party without his wife. I was the only one who believed there was no foretelling. But I remember when I, too, paid attention to symbols. I can't recall the beginning of when I stopped. And I no longer believe in the humility of monks.

THE CHASE

The footsteps she leaves are consistently interrupted by white lines as narrow as threads. You see them, then feel compelled to tilt your head upwards. You feel your brow compress into sutures as you consider the limpid light. The edges of your vision are rimmed in gold.

On one occasion, you walked the dusty streets of a forgotten town in Nepal. You passed through a storefront for the dimness you sensed would cool your shallow breaths. A man stepped forward from the shadows lingering on the walls. When he smiled, he blinded you with his teeth and you blinked. As your lashes fluttered open you saw a thin trail of smoke evaporating from the cup of tea immediately in your hand.

Let us discuss the passage of an hour, your mother once said. *Let us discuss how the tilt of a minute hand is both inconsequential and fraught with meaning. And*, your mother added after a silence fell like a wool cloak, *how the importance of an hour becomes relegated to the sound of each quiver from the hand on the face of an otherwise mute clock.* In response, your belly began to simmer and you asked faintly into the silence, *Mother: how did you come to speak like this?*

Over her footsteps, the edges of chiffon dresses once swayed with the breeze. Your favorite evoked rainbows and butterflies traipsing through rays of light. Once, she paused and turned to offer you an orange. You have never forgotten the experience of peeling away its thick hide—the remnants that would cling between the edges of your nails and skin. There were seeds, but you welcomed their bitterness to heighten the bursting sweetness of jasmine, of honeysuckle, against your tongue.

These memories are a single weight and you are the one with the extended palm, open and trusting the fall of light against the flesh that surrounds your life lines.

From the edge of your extended palm, air spills and as your gaze follows, you see her footsteps carefully straddling the thin excuse for a rope.

COME KNOCKING

You quirked an eyebrow when I said I loved the flag. What else can be summoned when you have never seen me drop a smile? Then you admired the cherries hanging from the ears of a lady behind me. But as I turned my back I felt you raise your hand before it sadly lapsed.

Someday we will discuss, you promised. It makes me order a drink. I know you admire encaustic for protecting forever the fragility of paper. But my friends begrudge you. Your blue shadows repel them. And they weep as I dive into the deep end.

I once rode an elephant through a field of tall grass. I laughed at a bear baring its yellow teeth. My guide was a pygmy who called me "Sir." My arms grew wiry tugging at rope. That evening, welts rose on my palms and I soothed them with the wet walls of a beer bottle.

What is the surface of reality? Do not our fathers matter? Life so transcends one's intention. With what are we grappling when we are not sleeping? Why need we grapple when we are dreaming? How difficult it must be for you. And still, I must come knocking

AFTER 2 A.M.

I have known complete rejection. The rain slid like a sheet falling against her white walls. I much preferred diamonds, enough to satiate craving. A wise artist suggested I look between raindrops. This, I determined, I could manage sideways. Sometimes, love simply leaves me replete.

You never leave that corner in my mind. You sit on a twin bed, its sheets impoverished, made in Bolivia. I often wonder how long your frail body can withstand the winds in America. Long ago, our adopted country unwound me like a courtesan evolving. But you are so much older than I am.

It is past 2 a.m. and you know what that means. I do not know with whom I am struggling in sweat-soaked sheets. I do not know if I am drowning. But when I wake to a new day, the blood on the walls scream for gilt frames.

I would love to see the tropics with you so I can save you from the bloodletting of mosquitoes. This, I would do simply by hovering. Fed on milk, my veins are always sweeter than what boils in natives clambering up coconut trees. Within those brown, hairy shells, the meat is rapturous and water pure. We know.

Do you laugh behind your closed door? When you hear me pleading, do your palms lift themselves of their own accord to lie against the cool walls of your monastery? It is impossible to unlock the armor encasing my heart. My blood is blue. You might as well reach for the brass blocking that keyhole

ADULTERY

       *   *

We met at an angle. You believed a certain science fiction tale about a universe whose citizens ran out of original ideas. It was disconcerting to conceive of someone feeling my heartbeat years before I opened my eyes for the first time. Between the first sense of my heartbeat and my eyes opening to light, how many lived and died? My chin folds into the bend of my neck as I consider, *How many thought to form wings?*

                            **

I know waves recede as secondary acts. Knowledge is inconsistent in lightening the burden of grief. Once, I reached forward to brush your hair away from the shimmer of your eyes. I did not expect to find an antique mirror. I did not expect you to feel the weight of your belief. I did not expect you to retain its unnecessary burden. This says as much about me as any concept we both can conceive. A thought might be fleeting but it still can scar deeply, even so efficiently as to leave an invisible wake.

                       **

Some mornings offer surcease with a faint tinkling of piano notes. The high notes thread their way through my pale blue veins. They make me arch my back as my cats do when they pause to look at me with disdain. They say before licking their fur, *You could never be one of us.* It only makes me begin to blubber and then feel relief at my loneliness as my face balloons into a red, ripe plum, the skin a mere thought away from splitting.

                    **

I know you were coming onto me full frontal. But we met at an apex. That I discover this only with hindsight does not make me begrudge our years together. But it does make me consider once more why mirrors and cameras make me uneasy unless I happen to duck my head or close my eyes. When my reflection is snagged, you see, I am drawn only to how startled I am. It is me walking a dark path and coming around the bend. Around the bend loom the lights of something big and bright threatening to run me off the road. In the scent of wet earth, the hold of dark leaves clinging to my ankles, the sound of fireflies mating, the thin sliver of a distant moon, there had been no premonition for such blinding light.

PROFILES

I returned to the wheat fields I had loved as a boy and realized I
was just beginning a transition, your friend said as his hair swayed
in the faint breeze. Behind him, a lone tree rose like an empty
flagpole to interrupt the horizon of a deserted beach. I looked at
him too intently because I was conscious of your hand an inch
away from mine. We shared a table whose span barely allowed the
width of a three-way conversation. He was your friend and I
detested my attempt to measure your intimacy.

Boulevards are at their best at night. The dimness caresses anyone
strolling past the lighted windows of locked stores. I could walk
forever down Broadway, then back again until I am eating a ripe
mango in Harlem. The music there is alien but I welcome the low
moaning of hidden throats. I try to avoid women's eyes as they
always make me cry.

I often recall Manila and the lost generation hugging the corners
of its streets. I believe many have forgotten how to look straight
ahead. And the women no longer wear their hair up. Their
President announces the improvement in the air, and he is
accurate. Still, most have lowered expectations.

Oh, Eileen, you have tiptoed down this path before. Why are you
now stepping deliberately on fallen branches, their sounds cracking
the air like the edges of blades against eggs? This must be what it
means to be a woman without sisters. For mothers must let go

COROLLA

Sometimes, I pray. Love is always haggled before it becomes. I clasp my hands around my disembodied truth: I am forever halved by edges—in group photos, on classroom seats, at mahogany dining tables whose lengths still fail to include me. I play myself perfectly, containing a Catholic hell within my silence to preserve the consolation of hope. *Hope*—once, I tipped Bing cherries into a blue bowl until I felt replete in the red overflow.

If my bones were hollow, like flutes made from reeds, I might savor the transcendence of Bach flowing through me rather than the fragile movement of marrow. "These are thoughts which occur only to those entranced by the layered auras of decay," my mother scolds me. I agree, but note the trend among artisans in sculpting prominent breasts on immobilized Virgin Marys. She replies, "But these are moments lifted out of context."

The green calyx emphasizes the burden of generously-watered corollas, though beauty can be emphasized from an opposite perspective. I have no use for calm seas, though I appreciate a *delicadeza* moonlight as much as any long-haired maiden. You see, my people are always hungry with an insistence found only in virgins or fools. It is my people's fate for focusing on reprieves instead of etched wrinkles on politicians' brows and mothers' cheeks. We are uncomfortable encouraging dust to rise.

I feel pain spread like wine staining silk—a gray wing, then grey sky. "Only God," I begin to whisper, before relenting to the tunes hummed by ladies with veiled eyes. The definition of holidays becomes the temporary diminishment of hostile noise. I do not wish to know what engenders fear from my father, even if it means I must simulate an aging beauty queen clutching photos of tilted crowns. I prefer to appreciate from a distance those points where land meets water: I prefer the position of an ignored chandelier.

When lucidity becomes too weighty, when the calyx sunders, I concede that I make decisions out of diluting my capacity for degradation. I frequently camouflage my body into a Christmas tree. I cannot afford to consider soot-faced children stumbling out of tunnels dug deep enough to plunge into China's womb. You say the rice cooker is flirting with its lid; I say, *I AM DROWNING IN AIR.* I have discovered the limitations of wantonness only in the act of listening. There is no value in negative space without the intuitive grid.

I am called "Balikbayan" because the girl in me is a country of rope hammocks and *waling-waling* orchids—a land with irresistible gravity because, in it, I forget the world's magnificent indifference. In this country, my grandmother's birthland, even the dead are never cold and I become a child at ease with trawling through rooms in the dark. In this land, throughout this archipelago, I am capable of silencing afternoons with a finger. In this country where citizens know better than to pick tomatoes green, smiling grandmothers unfurl my petals and begin the journey of pollen from anthers to ovary. There, stigma transcends the mark of shame or grief to be the willing recipient of gold-rimmed pollen. In my grandmother's country, votive lights are driven into dark cathedrals by the flames of *la luna naranja*, a blood-orange sun.

GREY, SURREPTITIOUSLY

Sometimes I am not tired. And I begin to pace the perimeter of
Manhattan. I am always drawn to the East River, how the water is
consistently grey and this sensibility mists over the entire East
Side: it swathes the total territory in a wool suit. And it makes me
recall interchangeable cities in Eastern Europe where the only
spots of color are offered by tiny pastries silently waiting behind
glass. Afterwards, I finish with memories of museum exhibits
salvaging dusty armors from the crusades of a different century.

I *am* surprised that I linger in this part of the city, that the river's
surface loses its drabness to enfold me like cashmere.
Unexpectedly, patchouli and cinnabar begin to linger in the air
though I see no one dodging my careful steps. I feel the birth of
pearls in tropical ocean beds tended by boys burnt by the sun.
Then I feel one pearl's inexplicable caress in the hollow between
my breasts.

A woman rounds a bend and sees me. I pause by a white birch
tree stripped by winter of its leaves. She smiles as she approaches.
I wish to feel my fingers loosening her jeweled combs. Already, I
can feel her hair curl shyly against my fingers like the breaking of
surreptitious surf. No words would be spoken, but a window
from an anonymous building would open to loosen the faint
tinkling of piano notes. They would be plucked from the highest
scale.

My fingers would turn blue in the cold. They would freeze in
their fraught pose, laid against a stranger's scented cheek while her
hair would continue to flutter in a faint breeze. And her lashes
would trap a beginning snow. And her life-generating breaths
would occur through parted lips. And her eyes, too, would be the
deadening of a river: translucent and grey.

NAMING LUCIDITY

A man nets leaves from a swimming pool. But the wind continues
to blow and the trees shake from its formless assault. On one
limb, a woman's long scarf is caught. It whips through the air like
a student's hand clamoring for attention. A man remains lost in
oblivion, netting one wet leaf after another. Soaked in chlorine,
each leaf has mottled. The shrivel of each is like blood clotting.

Is it a woman embraced by shadows who offers a haunting, a face
grieving a beloved scarf torn from her by a random wind? Red
lips open to release a sigh. A white hand reaches to caress a
marble throat. The nails are tipped by pale slivers of a waning
moon. Her lids inevitably lower. Before the lashes begin their
clinging, a stranger turns on the lights of a nearby house. In that
sudden luminosity, leashed tears glint. Soon, lashes shall darken
with a wet weight.

The invisible neighbor sees the woman shut her eyes and changes
his mind about obviating night. He dims his lights so that his
profile of observation will not be visible to the woman grieving
over yet another loss. Of their own accord, his fingers rise to rub
his chin. Once more, he feels the bristle from days of ignoring the
razor. He has been thinking dangerous thoughts whenever he
lifted the blade to his face. He is sufficiently lucid to know the
wisdom of recognizing when to halt certain practices until he can
stare into the mirror once more without wincing.

Years before the man first learned that one can flinch from a
mirror—oh, that honest reflection!—he was flirting with a
customer in a flower shop. He stopped by the florist to purchase
red roses for his mother. A lady admired his choice and marveled
at the delight the fragrant blooms undoubtedly would provide. He
tried to slip her one as he was sure his kind mother would
understand. She replied, *Nonsense!*—but accepted his invitation
to dinner. To begin that first date, he seated her before a table

clothed in cream damask and laden with silver and crystal. Then he asked her to close her eyes for a moment. In the darkness, she felt silk tantalize her naked throat. When she opened her eyes, a scarf embossed with red roses flowed over her breasts. She lifted her eyes to his watching smile.

THE COLOR OF A SCRATCH IN METAL

— after "Some Remarks on Color" by Enrique P. Barot

She was asked to imagine the taste of "silver, nickel, chrome"—or a scratch in them. The notion of the *scratch*, no matter how thin, evoked the taste of mercury. She is confident at the accuracy of her memory over an act that never occurred: she knows a broken thermometer would free the chemical that melted black Tahitian pearls. Light transforms their luster from black to grey. Like sunlight staining his black hair with a blue sheen. The thought makes her fingers quiet a raven as she strokes its throat, then wings.

If a pear was a color, she feels it would be how shadows glide across his unshaven chin. If honeysuckle was a color, she feels it would be how hatred or love lowers his lids. If passion was a color, she feels it would be the surface of black sand encasing the shores of a hidden beach on the other side of an ocean. Once, he took her there and, under the white heat of a noon sun, he flattened the helpless air surrounding her. That evening, her cheeks mirrored the crimson lashes against the sky as well as the inner flesh along her shifting thighs.

"And what is seeing?" Once, she asked him not to touch her hand as it laid next to his on white linen surrounded by crystal wine glasses, silver cutlery and purple lilies. It was a black tie affair and her dress was cut low, translucent in wise places and unabashedly luminous. He complied with her desire, even an hour later. But an hour later, she saw the sheen break across his forehead from the effort of keeping his hand frozen when what he desperately wanted to do was take her fragile fingers and crush them until she fell to her knees. And during the fall, she would have bared her throat. The tendon would have leapt. "And what is seeing?" It is how he saw her notice the strain of his effort but remained silent, offering no reprieve, so that the price he would extract later amidst twisted bed sheets would be high.

EULOGY

"we have never really left anywhere we have been"
— **Salman Rushdie**

"No movement independent of time"
— **Myung Mi Kim**

*

Yes, the day begins consistently with roosters lifting red, tufted heads and beaks clawing at air. Between their crescendos, I feel the sway of skirts as girls stoop to sweep away debris that night has cluttered throughout yards. It is another day in Santo Tomas, Philippines, and my thoughts recall my favorite part of Manhattan: a city skyline at night, their lights as far away from me as the stars but as near to me as the speed of light is intimate. Finally, and consistently, there is *you*: an embrace I feel across an archipelago. Desire is an ocean; there is no edge between us.

*

Losing uncertainty, we shared vitello tonato in a courtyard in Rome, the milky-white surface of the sauce camouflaging a peppery bite. You smiled as my fingers lined through the calmness of the Ganges while we watched pilgrims raise their eyes to dawn. When I saw daylight ripple silver across the surface of Lonoan Strait, I longed for you in Boston staring through snowflakes; I could feel your heartbeat against the palm I raised, askance, to block the sun. During your absence, I consider the concept of unity and come to believe—hope—that what lies beyond the horizon is the same gravity that loosens a woman's hair until a hue of blue might be seen in the wake of strands caressed by a man's breath. That same gravity unclenches a fist when thought halts and anger is dispelled. That same gravity obviates the furrows on a baby's brow when hunger abates. That same gravity always tugs at my breasts. That same gravity is the profile of the moon helplessly sliding between clouds. Your sideway glance is as tangible as the moment before a kiss.

*

The figures are dark against red clay and you love all of them. One man raises a sword at an enemy made invisible by the curvature of the vessel—and you especially like the disappearance. I prefer the dancer continuing to dance despite the presence of the warrior. Death is always limited by its failure to garner acceptance. You tell me, "I don't believe we can ever leave those we have met." Your tone lacks regret or foreboding, though you frequently warn against looking back. The past depends on how we control memory. Memory is a controlling agent. No one can discover what lies beyond an image without the progress of light. Fearlessly, hands reach forth to turn the vase around for another view. The blue vein leaps against the pale hide of a wrist encircled by a thin strand of gold. And your finger is tracing a vein, its protrusion helpless.

*

Radiation seduces me by bleaching bones into light. I consistently travel to search for what will touch off an implosion within my heart. The surface of a leaf dangling beyond my bedroom window is its own universe, I know, but I consistently travel. Through gritty desert air, I peered at a cliff dotted with dark burrows into the homes of ghosts. Unexpectedly, my loud greeting lacked an echo through the air over a deep canyon. With new respect, I looked at a nearby leaf and saw darkness camouflaging its edge. It has shriveled under the heat of light. The heat is as uncontrollable as what may surface from an inward search. That one begins a journey voluntarily will be irrelevant to the outcome? The source of a wave is never certain; despite its seeming repetition each wave is singular.

*

You say you met yourself in the dark moss climbing the pink walls of Alhambra surrounded by old hills where people have perfected suffering. To gaze into a steaming cup of tea sources comprehension on questions not yet asked. Or it may transcend that, or it may not, or it may depend on the definition of regret. Or, it may depend on comprehension's reliance on sight. Though the flame trees of Tambobo have emptied themselves to silver limbs clawing the sky, the orange blooms stain every sunset that would begin the dark hours of rumination. A blind member of the French Resistance insisted on learning dance to obviate the strange rhythm of alien boots and unfamiliar odor of tobacco colonizing Paris. A sunlit sensibility pervades dreams with ease, consistently. *"Now let us be fearless."*

THE BEGINNING

It was always like this: a journey out to the fringe of danger, then a quick and safe retreat. It seemed a pitiful surrender. The end of a barely-birthed millennium could be sighted, a foretelling that failed to categorize her mink coat as "old-fashioned." She was part of a different trend: walking the streets with Chopin plugging both ears.

Once, she slept for three nights in an otherwise empty hotel in Mindanao. The windows opened onto a terrace that the bellhop suggested she avoid. *Not that you are a fat lady*, the bellhop added belatedly with a nervous giggle. She looked at him for the first time and noticed he was old enough to be her grandfather. She decided to become content with the views behind glass of a sea patrolled by wooden boats festooned with colorful masts. She felt she should have a memory of fishermen's wives stitching together cloths of white for clouds, red for birds, yellow for suns and blue for skies. With composure, she understood that it would be remnants that would create rainbows. The masts waved as if they were unraveling, letting in too much wind through holes left behind by oversized needles. Still, they satisfied fishermen who only trawled by the shore. For adventures closer to the distant horizon, they replaced sails with noisy motors. She could hear the rusty motors breathing awkwardly through their paces, churning salt in the water.

She knew an island existed beyond her vision, past where the earth continued the downward trend of its arc. On that island, she knew more than one man thought of her. She knew they could not imagine what she saw everyday: glass on skyscrapers that stunned her with her aging reflections. Or, that when she sees through transparent walls, she sees old men huddled over street grates or old women pushing stolen shopping carts laden with useless debris—like knife handles with no blades, novels missing their last pages or seeds that will never feel the embrace of warm, wet earth.

For a moment, she wondered what it would have been like to be a slave girl during the thirteenth century in an arid land. She envisioned the sky overhead to have been a dirty brown and the sun a flickering yellow globe. Her breasts, most assuredly, would have bared themselves to anyone's stare. Her wonder occurred for only a moment, lasting like a single flicker of a hummingbird's wings.

She knew her lover's best friend was in love with her, and that all of his failed relationships derived from his search for oblivion. He knew she will never leave her lover, though she considered fidelity irrelevant. She wondered about what her lover's best friend did understand: serial killers and their perpetual propensities. She considered lack of control unseemly—and that *this* was the trait that distracted men into falling in love with her facade. Yes, she knew that, out of control, she would be glorious. She knew the danger of her lover never ever having seen her lose.

For their tenth anniversary, her lover gave her an expensive oil portrait of a woman unknown to them. *But the paint transcends her identity*, they agreed. In the beginning, she also considered the stranger's face to be the homeliest woman she had ever witnessed. When she woke up one day and discovered beauty in the stranger's lined brows, unsmiling gaze, wrinkled cheeks and thin lips, she began to question her collection of assumptions. Months passed before she woke up another day to the wish that she had been a kind person during her past. Kindness, she believed, could have transcended much that was visible and much that was not.

THE SOULFUL UNIVERSE

— for Kathleen Chang and Meister Eckhart

She picks pink chiffon whose sleeves are embroidered with white dandelions. Her long skirt flutters in the breeze and you smell honeysuckle. She kisses your brow with her eyes before reaching for a container by her naked feet. You are still smelling honey as she douses herself. And you believe you are in a dream when she lights a match and sets herself on fire. You run toward her but the glass wall halts your stride. As your palms flatten against the invisible but implacable border, you feel her say before pink chiffon disappears in a blaze, *Let there be grace.*

"But what if it turns out that the laws of physics aren't so fixed and invariable after all? What if the universe makes its own laws just as it makes space and time?"

A gypsy persistently tracks me up and down Broadway. She has come to know which are my favorite cafes. She begs, *Please, may I speak to you about the radiance of your face?* I do not disagree with her sighting a halo's shadow against my cheek. I simply wish not to witness her fall when my lack of need, inevitably, makes her weep.

"Now suppose that the law of physics the new universe inherited could differ slightly from the laws in its parent universe? If these changes affected the production of black holes, then over many cycles a kind of Darwinian pressure would encourage the formation of universes whose physics favored black holes, since universes that did not make black holes would have no progeny."

Let there be grace, you heard her say. And you begin to recall her calls for renouncing materiality. Black holes may be found when stars burn out and collapse under their own weight—in the ensuing space, the density of mass and energy become infinite. But why be surprised if infinity has a body, or if it is an organ? Consequently, you hold back your tears. Through their silver shimmer, you begin to understand her *Idealism*: the morality of detachment that transcends mere ascetism. Once, she stumbled across an ancient photo of an ascetic: in eyes hollowed by hunger, an infinite ecstasy

THE WIRE SCULPTURE

— after Richard Tuttle's sculptures of pencil, wall, wire, shadows, nail, space

The shadow is thin but what slices air is thinner. The press
of approximation is confidently approximate. It does not matter
to the naked eye. What is solid is what is not visible. Once
more, you look back at the sculpture. But the light has changed
with the progress of the hour. You leave and dwell instead on the
simmer deep within your belly. How a shadow's imperfection
humbles you. How a shadow recalls a life you once wanted to
possess versus the life that folds itself around your awkward
steps.

THE FROZEN GASP

She sent him a letter containing the observation, *It is so difficult
to differentiate between insanity or saintliness.* Against the
stationery's pale blue, the words gestured shards from night. He
felt her sitting in a shuttered room, with her hands like moving
stalagmites as they scribbled furiously under the russet beam of an
ancient lamp. Inevitably, she would have paused to rub a knuckle
against her eyes, and he felt that, too: the fist helplessly clenched,
straining against the blindness of lashes clinging desperately
together.

He considers himself a "civilized" man. He has never betrayed a
woman without first ensuring her joy in the aftermath.
Sometimes, a single rose at the height of perfume accomplished
the task. Other times, the task required carats of emeralds, rubies
and sapphires. He never begrudged. Still, he wonders how long
he must continue with the diamond solitaire he maintains in
reserve. He would like to take it out of its black velvet box where
it, too, lies breathless with anticipation. He feels the stone frozen
in a gasp.

Once, a different lady passed through the perimeter of his sight.
She had been sheathed in a velvet dress whose narrow skirt sliced
open between her thighs. The fold had opened with her first step
towards him, and never again fully closed. He will never forget
the black silk that encased her limbs. Its glimmer approximated
the surface of her eyes when he left and she refused to cry. This
is a paragraph he articulates in hindsight.

He lays the blue letter flat against the burnished leather stretched
atop his mahogany desk. Nearby, a crystal dish offers a stack of
business cards. They identify him innocuously. Despite their
raised letters on thick, cream vellum, the cards are specious. A
gentleman is always more than the coincidence of a name
allocated without his consent. A gentleman never needs a title,

especially one that qualifies *President* with *Vice.* He realizes all this as he flattens his fingers against a silk tie. Despite the rhythm of geometric patterns that would trap an observer's watch, the tie's surface is slippery. It is facile.

THE EMPTY FLAGPOLE

The shifting relationship between the senses and the intelligence makes the apprehension of reality problematic, even when one repeatedly refuses, as [Jasper] Johns does, to succumb to the desire for asylum.
— *from* **The United States of Jasper Johns** *by* **John Yau**

What does it say about me when I ask for asylum in places where people wish to leave? I try to find meaning in flags. But they repel me when buffeted by an incidental breeze. Oh, I reconsider when I am pierced by an empty flagpole. It makes me think of barkers at street corners flaying the wake of traffic. They should never sell their souls.

There I go again with sideway glances. I do not need a mirror to know my reflection. When I close my eyes, the sensation is home made, deep dish apple pie. I forget that I deliberately failed to sign the checks I mailed. Must even the tiniest ant get a bite?

I try to get by but show up in clown outfits where others deconstruct black dresses. Once, I actually threatened to bear someone's child. This evening I walked exactly 100 long blocks in New York City. On Block No. 99, a redhead with hair trapped in corn rows ruined me with an approach. It didn't matter that the offer was a drug store sale proclaimed by a cheap flyer. I was accosted by desire.

Sometimes I get tired of immolation. And I haven't slept for a while. How I long for another stranger to relish my lips.

APPROXIMATIONS

She deliberately wears a dress that exposes the sharpened blades of her shoulders and the gold wires piercing her navel. She knows their stares linger, that they wish to dip their gazes lower. No one ever credits her with replacing the mask of solitude with something else. She is judged by the amorality of tearing off the jeweled combs that caged her hair. They believe her to be her red velvet dress, cut, too, to reveal a melting ziggurat when she ripples a muscle along her thigh.

He refuses to understand why she would leave amidst their state of bliss. When she replies by praising the shell of a cathedral in Barcelona that men failed to complete despite the passing of an entire century, she knows her explanation cannot be clearer. She can feel the workmen's roughened hands, gritty with dust, as they cracked yet another slab of marble. She wishes to be all of the women awaiting their return each evening. They would cross thresholds desperate for tubs of steaming water. Afterwards, they would turn first to her before bread, cheese and wine. As shadows darkened, she would feel their rough hands tremble in their approximations of gentleness.

She once found cruelty by cashing in a rare ticket to the fashion shows of Paris. She spent subsequent decades seeking to return. But the earth continued to spin and she has never mastered how to rupture a circle's smooth bend. Then a woman passed through a small town in the Midwest where she stayed for a summer. (She can never remember the name of this town she felt compelled to taste because it has never been desired: its people always left.) The woman recalled how difficult it was to overcome years of ballet training. *I would rather dance the flamenco: always, the back must be straight no matter how hard the feet stomps to cleave the earth.* The woman obviated Paris. Still, she did not expect her heart to be sundered by the sight of the woman's hair in the wake of her departure. It was tossed carelessly by a harsh wind.

Now, she is distracted by a new man because she knows it is merely a matter of time before he flees. She considers her goal to be modest: that breezes contain themselves during the day he departs. When he leaves, she wishes that day to be sunlit and the horizon a clean line. She hopes to memorize the shadow of his departure cutting neatly across the horizon. She does not want a random wind to blur the edges of that memory she will slip into a plastic-encased page in a sterilized photo album. Resignedly, the album always waits. It is covered by pictures of flowers in full bloom, resplendent in sight despite their lack of perfume.

JULIET'S SALT

She is trying to persuade you that salt is sensual. Like the girl-
toddler she spotted walking along the edge of a dusty Midwest
road. She says the girl was naked except for a green wool blanket
dangling off one shoulder. Most of all, she says, she recalls the
girl's curly, red hair flowing down past her knees. Nearby, an azure
butterfly. You can feel the scene that she's lost in. It is the same
moment of regret you feel when you say something cruel to your
father, and, to your surprise, he merely turns to leave the room in
silence. His face is impassive, but it clutches at your heart. You
raise your hand against the sight of his receding back. Your chest
will not stop heaving. And, for a histrionic minute, you wish to
die.

Oh, Juliet, you lied. Salt is sensual, but you (are) still
compromised. I'll see you in that dim saloon down the road. I
know my breasts will not be cupped in red satin. No feathers in
my hair, fishnet up my thighs. I'll be in buckskin with a healthy
stallion waiting outside. And with my poker winnings, I'll do more
than survive. I'll pick up the bar tab while you leash your tears
and reach for my hide. Salt stings what will hide behind your
smiles. Oh, Juliet: those black lies!

JANUARY

The roses have emptied their vase. A week has lapsed since their stems were spliced before entering the crystal she topped with water and two teaspoons of sugar. The roses bloomed when she wasn't looking. But when she looked, their petals were brittle and mute. She marveled that not a single petal had fallen.

Last year, she received a crate of pears. That the sender hid his or her identity didn't matter after the few minutes of interrogating the mumbling messenger. She could still feel the thick juice dripping down her chin. She could see the pale green skin lightly flecked with what could have been gold dust. Finally, it was Christmas and there were pine wreaths tied up in red satin bows hanging about the room. A new year began just yesterday but the wreaths still remained, scenting the light.

Once, she bought a rug from a man in a turban. Bombay bustled beyond the short, doorless entryway into the man's store. She could hear the rickety wheel of a rickshaw, the laughter of a child, the scolding by a mother-in-law and the dust puffing up in the air from a runner's kick. The rug was patterned in small squares with crimson, orange and blue thread. The man suggested she hang it on a wall as it was woven out of silk. Back in New York, she decided she liked her toes fondling its weave. It was the first time her toes experienced bliss.

Yesterday, she read her first book that castigated the Roman empire. She had not realized that Christians also had ordered men to be thrown to the lions; even if the victims were pagans, she had not known that Christians, too, had been entertained by lions cracking human bones. She raised her eyes from the gilded page of the leather-bound book and caught her surprise in a cracked mirror across the room. Her eyes were wide and anguished. She knew she was not really pained by something that had happened so many centuries ago. The newly-ended year was still folded about her heart.

The most generous gift she received during the holidays was trapped in black velvet within a blue box bow-tied by a silver ribbon. It was from a corporation. *So,* she thought with the wonder of discovery as she picked up the silver pen embossed with her initials, *I was never forgiven after all for my first lie.* Sadly, she thought she would have preferred a pair of discreet earrings, or a locket holding a black-and-white portrait, or a bracelet, or an exceedingly modest charm for a bracelet. She remembered visiting the United Nations early on Christmas day. She thought watching the flags of many nations wave in the breeze would be soothing. But the flagpoles were empty in the winter chill, rising like poorly lit pencils held up to interrupt the skyline across the frozen river.

Bereft, she laid her entire body against the length of the silk rug flattened in the mahogany-paneled foyer. She felt the cold hardness of marble. She breathed in the pine scent of wreaths and wondered how long they would last. Bereft, she closed her eyes. In the darkness, she saw roses bloom for the first time, and they were an exquisite vermilion.

FIREBIRD

Perhaps I could silence this firebird *swelling my sails with blood winds, fevers, but even the Seine today was restless.*
— from Nearer the moon *by Anais Nin*

Broadway clamored for her attention. A wet mist diffused the boulevard's lights. One road grappled north, the other south. In the darkness, hands appeared and disappeared, their movements lacking premonition. Some bore ragged paper cups for her favors; others bore folded currency for other types of favors. Once, a hand revealed elegant, red fingernails and she almost halted her firm stride through night.

A woman sang sadly into the earphones plugging both ears. *Ecstasies,* she once read, *are too rare.* But it was not happiness that lingered on the street she savored for its camouflage of crowds. There was no bitterness in her recognition. The destination, she recognized, would arrive at its own time, indifferent to organization. Life is generous with consistent surprises.

Before a red light, she chose to recall her memories of Rome. She had walked for hours searching for a restaurant hidden behind high stone walls. When she found it, she stepped onto a small area with censored lamps, light coming only from the glare of pristine white tablecloths reflecting an orange moon. When she was seated, she was the only woman there. The scent of cigars permeated the air. The Chianti was harsh on the palate. But she savored each bite of her bleeding steak, and the men left her alone. For these pleasures, she effortlessly held her spine straight.

Back in New York, she paused before a man's bowed back. Despite the dimness and the clinging mist, he kept painting the tango on a panel of the sidewalk. She could see the flare of the woman's skirt as the man shifted its direction. She could see the jealous faces of women seated among a watchful crowd—the resentment of the men attending them. The artist had not yet painted in the couple's faces, but she knew they would be stunning. She knew the woman's teeth would be white, the lips stained crimson. She felt the woman licking her lips, the thickened tongue sliding languorously.

TRAVELER

Sometimes, the smallest things are enough to make her rhapsodize. She recalls looking over a stranger's shoulder and the cover of his book winking at her. Its blue was as vivid as what she now sees. Bound by mere string, she is lounging atop a white yacht floating on the Aegean Sea. Bronzed men move busily and they are all beneath her. Except for one with white hair and green eyes who climbs a gleaming steel ladder to offer opened figs sprawled on ice.

He believes *Identity* cannot be fixed. She wonders if that means *Self* must be fragmented. The air is warm. She recalls another man whose goal is an impermeable world. "What is compassion?" Once more she asks as she ignores the unexpected force to cry. Must desire always entail a loss of innocence? Figs stain her fingers purple and, slowly, eyes closed, she suckles them: one by one.

The horizon intrudes with a dying sun. Her blood rushes at the sky's acceptance of red. Another man beset by a scar slashed across his cheek offers her a silk robe. She slips into it with gratitude and allows the linger of his gaze. Suddenly, a string of lights blaze overhead to outline the masts. She feels she might as well be looking at New York City's skyline and wonders whether, just once, just once, her lips have ever formed the words to define *Home*.

SECOND PLACE

The surface of the *cafe au lait* has become a knothole. Then she understands how long she has tarried. She doesn't even like sitting on hardened plastic, though the booth is scarlet. She turns her face towards the waiters' section but it is as empty as her succeeding thoughts. So she turns her eyes towards the window. The glass offers a reflection of her gaze: an inconclusive destination.

A shadow hovers over the flat of her table but she refuses to pay attention. She knows the dim shape bobbing is the fake cowboy who had leered all evening from the counter. Her eyes begin to crack, like hurt eggshells. She thought she had learned control by now but her best intentions continue not to suffice. When the cowboy moves on with a muttered oath about the bathroom's location, it fails to provide consolation.

She does not believe it more than a modest goal: this search for "consolation." She gave up on redemption long ago. The occupant of a birdcage besides her table begins to sing. She decides to try once more, but after she looks up with a smile she sees the bird is crooning towards the window where its reflection is most receptive with the image of a corresponding song. Once more, she feels betrayed by illusion. This is how she came to sit in an obscure diner, in plastic that repels her. This is how she came to ignore *cafe au lait* until it jelled into the surface of an interior flaw. She assumes nothing has changed its creamy feel along the edges of her tongue. But she feels that in its long, warm slide down her throat there no longer will be a mother's comfort, even as she would be forced to swallow.

LIES

He asked her a question about love. He failed to camouflage his
true intent. She sought to soothe him by responding literally. It
was not until months collapsed before she realized how a mere
affirmation would have been the kindest gesture of all. Once
more, she was buffeted by her failure to accomplish what would
have been so simple a task.

She visited San Francisco during the last year of a briefcase
clinging to her hand. She stayed in a gilded hotel overlooking a
square park whose trees and benches domesticized the lonely. She
heard the hotel concierge's advice, even paused in the midst of a
Persian rug to turn it over in her mind as if it was a book with
velvet covers, compelling perusal. Then she loosened the advice
from her thoughts as a small piece of debris she could and did
deposit into one of the crystal ashtrays winking under the lights of
the hotel lobby's ten chandeliers. "Inhale / Exhale." Then she
walked to the park and sat on a bench, long after the mist
transformed itself into rain.

*I just returned from jogging four-and-a-half miles in the winter
chill,* she chirped over the phone the following morning. Damp-
eyed, she would have preferred to say, *I'm just returning from
Tunisia—how jovial it was!* After she answered his question and
both agreed to see each other soon, she looked at the telephone
and wondered why she felt incapable of lying to him. Is it the lie
or him? Uncertain, she paused to search her memory of her
current self: has she uttered a lie recently?

Last year, she ended one night's sleep with the command to recall
and enumerate over breakfast her favorites among his traits. She
began with the gold-rimmed emeralds that passed for his eyes,
how he anticipated her longings for solitude and food, the
wideness of his ambition, the scope of his intellect and, most of
all, his lack of fear. If she ever bore children, she knew she would

do so only for him: fearless, green-eyed lawyers. She was confident that one would become President of the United States. She paused to sip her tea and glanced at the window. Watching her, her reflection on unshakeable glass proclaimed, *You silly girl. You are going to end up alone, alone, alone.*

NOBILITY

. . . as a wave is a force and not the water of which it is composed, . . .
so nobility is a force and not the manifestations of which it is composed . . . .
— Wallace Stevens

She opens her silk robe before lying, face down, on the stone floor. The surface is rough against her breasts, cold against her brow. Her tears do not help. She wills herself in that position for the hours that her adoring public believes she wallows in a bubble bath (champagne and strawberries presumably within reach). Suffering never counts when it is shared.

After chaining a diamond necklace around her neck, her lover walked out of the door. She never saw him again, and will recall forever how he never broke his stride with a single look back. Diamonds never complete a bed. She sheathed herself in a black gown trimmed by purple feathers and ordered a limousine towards Long Island. Digging her satin pumps into the sand, she flung the diamond necklace over the surf as if she pitied a mermaid pleading for it. She did not begin her chosen act with the presumption of a prayer. Introductions are inherently insufficient.

She no longer questions why the fall of snow reminds her of Africa. She once straddled a man there for the access to his blanket woven from threads dyed in brilliant hues of red, blue, green and yellow. The fabric was gritty against her knees and she welcomed that more than the clench of his teeth below her breasts. She was determined to live out the rest of her life in technicolor. In New York, the snow is never pure. She likes the effect of contamination on white.

Nor has she experienced surprise since a young poet told her that he writes from "a position of happiness." *It is my way of continuing tradition*, he said calmly, *and is very much an aesthetic consideration.* When she dropped her eyes before the stark nudity of his sincerity, her gaze snagged on the ending of a poem he was offering from an outstretched hand. The young poet's words concluded: *The physical reality of revolution is decadence. The aftermath is what transcends.*

ASTHMA

Though the panes are crafted from capiz shells gathered from a sea's bounty, his windows hover over an urban canyon that has never been shadowed by an eagle's flared wings. She feels what he sees: the lack of a mountain's jade face. Traversed by a river flowing like my tears silvered by moonshine. Whose salt etched my cheeks when I watched an ocean seduce him. We share a fate perpetually revolving around water. Whose liquidity cannot cohere. Into a body one touches to ignite desire and a long-forgotten memory. We are consistent in our urges to continue traveling as if *Home* exists. Thus, awaits.

He is humming a song about obsidian-eyed children whose tribal names have been sacrificed to evolve a new race: carbon-breathers. He observes that the lead content in our people's blood is as high as those suspended within the citizens of ancient Rome. "Drinking wine in lead cups lowered their I.Q.'s." He strums a guitar as he concludes: feeding Christians to lions became inevitable.

She cannot compromise now by confusing her pronouns when she replies, "You make me remember an old poem where I was aghast to discover that Christians also fed humans to animals they first starved." In turn, he recalls his fear of carnal sin. She remembers that same conversation. About angels falling on wet, jagged boulders to the opera of lightning and thunder. Plummeting to own their vision instead of seeing through God's lenses. She had shared what a different man had taught her: "Fear is not a productive Muse." She does not tell him that to master the lesson, she had worn a blindfold before bending. Nor does she tell him that she learned that lesson, not because she loved its teacher but, because she was curious about its fable that lurked in a book entitled *PURITY.*

He mentions the difficulty of breathing in a place saturated with dinosaurs' ghosts, where the sky has forgotten the color of sunlit cobalt. That must affect your singing, she thinks, but surprises herself when the words she loosens are: "You are weeping for your people and yourself." She attempts self-control, only to fail when she adds, "But it's nice to have someone to cry for." Both recognize her slip as her latest acknowledgment that his departure turned her blood into dust. Turned her breath into ice.

She believes he is kind when he ignores her confession. That he kindly changed the subject by sharing a physician's theory that "asthma" is engendered by an inability to cry. That wheezing sounds are caused by unshed tears. However, he offers a different version: unshed tears are like coal: "Unmined. Unburnt. Heat waiting to happen."

She ran away from his tangible flesh in cyberspace, only to realize the error of her analysis. He had not ignored her confession. He had articulated a stone's potential to glow. To burn. To conflagrate. Like the first gaze they shared. Like the tendons of his thigh pressing against her palm. Like his thumbs pressing into her waist. Like his lips skimming across a jutting bone. Water, she suddenly remembers, can do more than evaporate. As she jogs through the park sweetly-scented by pollinating bees, under a sunset crimsoning a lapis lazuli sky that ended a storm, she realizes he will return to her. That the ocean his feet skims wraps around a globe. That the globe is a circle. That it lacks a seam to mark a beginning or an end. All this, before passion. All of this, before *Passion*.

BLIND DATE

You had seen him before but thought the prior sighting inconsequential. Then he was walking through the door to your brother's party. You were serving drinks to repay the debt incurred to your mischievous brother when you bluffed during rounds of poker. You lowered your lashes as you offered a tray of silver-rimmed flutes bearing what your brother called "an insouciant sancerre."

You could feel his gaze like the weight of fingertips tracing the edges of your publicly sanguine lips. You could sense the dust motes dancing through beams thrown by a sconce clinging to a papered wall.

Your brother approached with much cheer and he might as well have been rubbing his hands. You tried to leave with your tray but your brother stopped you with an introduction. *This is Mark. Mark, this is my stubborn sister.* You looked at Mark directly for the first time. What you saw parted your lips. Your mischievous brother watched you suspend breathing, took away your tray, and gave you glass. He left with even more cheer.

Why are you stubborn? he asked just as you said, *I am not stubborn.* Both of you were supposed to sense the presence of a B-movie camera, thus, smile after this overlap. Instead, he watched you drop your gaze to the vein on his neck leaping wildly beneath his impassive face. You turned to walk away but he raised a hand to block your path. *Your brother promised me a sunset,* he said, motioning towards the other end of the living room. A wide window waited, framed with violet velvet curtains.

I didn't lose that badly in poker, you replied but moved to where Mark requested. You assumed he understood the reference. You could feel his unblinking stare. He might as well have spanned your waist with one hand. As you approached the window a shadow flitted across the pane. It made your steps falter but he whispered reassuringly, *It's only an eagle*. Then you moved quickly towards the window to see the bird, but all you could see was a green feather falling. Or, was it the Chinese universe of a leaf?

Once, your mother called you in the middle of the night. *I just had a feeling you were troubled*, she said, panicked. You soothed her back to sleep with reassurances and silly jokes. After you hung up the phone, you went to your bathroom mirror and looked at your reflection. Your face was ripe. Against this memory, you sipped wine for the first time that day. The cold liquid and its warmth down your throat brought you forward to the present where a familiar stranger was peeling away your thoughts.

You could feel Mark watching you instead of the view beyond the window. The sun began to set and you felt its departure skim across your face. When city lights began to dot the darkness, you looked at him and said, *Violet is a tricky color. It is most effective as a stain.*

He responded by taking the folds of the curtain and, before you could grasp his intent, swaddled it around you as if you were an infant. *Even violet can be gentle*, he said before gently placing a swatch by your cheek. The velvet was soft and, against your control, you leaned closer towards it. You rubbed against his covered fingers. Beneath the velvet, his fingers trembled and you knew he was struggling to remain still. When you, finally, laid your lips against his, it was an appropriate thing to do so that civilization could continue.

HOW CYBERSPACE LOST MIDNIGHT

Petals cling to the wet pavement, forlorn in their solitude and with the insistence of their grasp. She tries to avoid stepping on them, then considers the intention silly. But she continues to avoid their pale flesh, seeking instead the stolid indifference of the pavement. In the fragility of a cyclamen's aftermath, she senses a storm's apology.

She is familiar with departures: the loosening of embraces, the forfeiture of birthplaces. One more tick across the clock's face and a new day would begin—the end of day in darkness, the beginning of a new day in the same darkness...so it must have been with French poets when it was a difficult century.

She has stared into a certain monk's face. When he smiled at her, the small huts, the large bells, the whiskered goats and the gnarled trees disappeared until all she saw was the monk's body interrupting the charred horizon. She thought that if she looked down at their feet, she only would see their sandals anchored inexplicably on air. She didn't look down. She held on to the monk's smile until a piece of his red robe fluttered and distracted her gaze towards the cotton so soft she felt it might as well have been silk. She did not need to touch the fabric to feel it skim lightly across her cheek and provide welcome consolation.

Before the millennium, this thing called the Internet sought to intervene. It might be a black hole. With every e-mail message, it cackles, *I am where no man has gone before.* Emily Post is dead in the Internet. Within cyberspace, once appetite is satiated no time remains for laying the fork and knife side by side across the plate of bone china. This thing called the Internet has eliminated insomnia. In the ensuing blur of meaning, she launches a message through the black hole that will make poets across an entire continent reply with agitated fingers, *Do your lovers beat you?* She wrinkles her brow in understanding for the first time how much she is about to lose, even as she refuses to pull the emergency rope that would cease the train she discovers herself piloting. There are bodies laid on the tracks.

UNSAID

I know you prefer them younger and of a different sex. I will
swallow all that. I paint my face if I know I will stumble over you
hugging a street grate over a subway tunnel. When I bend my face
and feel the grit from the flight of a train, I welcome the caress in
the absence of your hands reaching for my ribcage. Finally, I will
have left all underwear home.

Sometimes you complain about the gas bill. That hurls me to my
knees. If I could save you from a faceless utility, I'd strip off my
mask. Yes, I'd offer you the ripest plum, ready to split apart from
a thought. The seed easily would fall off, roll to a corner of the
room and gather dust. I still would be folded about your tongue.

Once, your hand laid a breath away from mine on an unsuspecting
table top. A typhoon made my hairs stand on end. My face must
have mirrored the fall of antique hair. I do know my lips had
cracked like a parched desert under a cowboy's sun. Yet my teeth
shivered, each a lonely individual assaulted by one-night stands.

I get so tired sometimes. But your most single of coughs always
makes me run. I wish to be air so you can stride through me, lean
through me, simply face me—whatever suits you. I long for the
day when you bring me mint tea, from a bag and the water fresh
from an impoverished microwave. I long, not for the tea but your
hand approaching me generously—purposefully. I would let the
steam linger between us to memorize your stance of an offer, even
as I know your gaze would be blank.

Yes,   I get so tired sometimes

THE INVESTMENT BANKER

*

Lime coats the thick sheaf of paper crossed by thin, parallel lines
of a darker green. They approximate the rippling surface of a
river pregnant with water and smoothly traveling towards an orb
of sea salt. His pen is a black crow against a sunlit sky. Its ink is
harsh, blotting paper, even with the neat economy of motion in
how the ink is laid. For a moment, a golden spark glints from a
cufflink struck by a sun ray. Meticulously, the ink travels from
point to point, dipping, then rising, then dipping again until it is
halted by one of the four walls of a square. The paper mottles.
He lays the pen besides the projection of a likelihood as an ache
begins between his shoulder blades. As he rolls his head in a
circle, he considers the placement of a decimal point. Lastly, he
considers the definition of a percentage to be the probability of
error instead of the probability of an answer's relevance.

*

It seems a secretary with large hair is shuffling until he notices
that it is only a tight skirt hampering her thighs. He begins to feel
the papers stacked on a crudenza curling their edges to protest
being ignored. A lock of hair falls in front of his eyeballs and he
notices a white feather. He immediately comprehends how long it
has been since scissors tip-toed about his scalp. Bereft, he looks at
his desk and is astonished at how still his fingers lie atop a yellow
pad—he would have sworn his fear would have left his empty
palms quaking at how time is consistently ending.

*

He looks up to be surprised at midnight "a done deal." His hands
seek release and he wipes them against the pin-striped wool
encasing his thighs. A woman with a blurred face atop a blue silk
shirt pops her head through the door. He knows she is speaking

but his gaze cannot locate the source of the buzzing. He feels a fleeting thought of inebriated bees, how they might blunder with pollen gratuitously. His gaze falls to the circle of diamonds on her left, blue-veined wrist. He takes a chance and replies, "Yes." It is sufficient to make her go away so that all that remains across his threshold is the shadow of a door. He feels he must complete the job by shutting a door but he is so tired.

*

Was I ever a boy? he asks himself as he watches the Chairman hold hands with his tall wife. The wife smiles but it is clear she is dangling her legs over a pedestal. When he reaches them for an obligatory greeting, he realizes (without being surprised at the certainty of this thought) that she smells expensive. He hears her emerald earrings tinkle like wind chimes. His breath is the breeze against her pale, seamless skin. She smiles at him and he feels even smaller. His breath is the flutter of a Trochilidae's wings. When he next turns to the Chairman, he is buffeted by the Chairman's smug grin.

*

He tattoos his fingerprints on the most random of surfaces. It happens that way each morning when he must read six newspapers beside The *Wall Street Journal.* One is in Japanese. Another in German. He cannot recall the last time he was lucid. He cuts himself shaving whenever the mirror reminds him that his eyes are covered by red cracks. They remind him of bigger faultlines just waiting to widen. He knows he will fold into himself during the fall. He feels that avoidance should be under his control. But it is not happening and he is often immobilized by this failure.

*

I should fall in love, he thinks, as he reads a worn newspaper clipping. It has traveled throughout the firm and reached him last. He flinches at the leers clinging to the message. His fingers feel wet though the clipping is dry. The clipping is about Alan "Swift" Thiessen, the man who once sat in an office down the hall. Once, Swift was a tight muscle tightly sheathed in Italian suits with double-breasted blazers, a sartorial sun amidst the human commodities forging together a partnership. It was an eccentricity allowed by Swift's ability to bleed rain from desiccated clients. Once, Swift also played squash every day. Now, Swift is clad in rough cotton and measures each passing moment in a jail, staring at rust and bricks. The newspaper reports how Swift went too far with a young, blonde boy sheathed in leather with metal studs. Still, The Investment Banker suggests to himself that he fall in love. Despite Swift's ignominious end, he feels that Swift still bested him by having felt certain compulsions about which he can only remain curious.

*

At 4 a.m. he is not displeased to be alone walking the streets. At 4 a.m., he feels that the hour offers a certain excuse for his loneliness. Now, he is walking in the aftermath of an unseasonal rain so that the light is clean and the pavement shines from the wash of water. The tall buildings conspire to maintain sufficient lights to surround him like Christmas. He notices a white flower in a bud vase by a window he passes. It is unexpected but pleasing and he pauses to think, *Hello!* He knows he is imagining things but he senses the flower open its petals a tad wider. His nostrils flare at the inexplicable perfume of jasmine. He looks forward to winter when snow will cover the city. Even in a blizzard, the snow is constant. They never fail to cling softly to him as he walks in their midst. He feels, *It is such a loving feeling.*

THE SECRET OF HER HAPPINESS

The cafe was crowded, too loud, and the window by her table opened to an argument between a mother and daughter. Both were too old to be using the tones they were slinging at each other. Her waitress wore an apron that had not been washed for weeks. She felt her hand clutch a utensil and looked down. She bathed in relief over the spotless ellipsis of a spoon.

She ordered steamed eggs with a mixture of parsley, mint, oregano and basil. The description of the dish was histrionic and she bowed to curiosity. All she had wanted was black coffee and plain oatmeal in skim milk. The menu advised that if she also ordered a scone with sour cream and apple jelly, she would have succeeded in ordering a "British Breakfast." Between that and ordering cappuccino instead of black coffee, she sniffed and made a choice to avoid exhaustion. Like the old days, the British won.

She opened her bag but couldn't find a Russian novel. She thought of writing a letter. She wished she was reading a handwritten letter. The eggs arrived and she thought of salt's immense pleasure. Dave Brubeck played the piano in her ears. With gratitude, she observed the mother and daughter walk away. When she saw them pause to hug each other, she noticed the sky was blue, the sun shining and a new waitress on duty.

The first time she discovered happiness, it was inappropriate. She realized concurrently her mother would never enjoy the same discovery. In the immediate wake of that revelation, she had been confused over what was more startling: that her mother was incapable of something or that her mother was doomed to sadness. No matter how often she would kiss and embrace her mother, her mother's fate would not change. The year of this revelation also provided the first time Christmas failed to become a distraction.

Once, she felled her mother to her knees. She was sixteen and stood on a stool wearing a pink polyester dress whose stiff lace irritated her neck. Her mother bowed her head as she carefully pinned the dress to shorten its hem. She remembered looking down at her mother and noticing for the first time a hairless area of scalp. Her mother had never seemed so naked. Yet she had stayed the involuntary gesture of her hand to reach forward and raise her mother from her knees—to empty her mother's mouth of pins.

She has not yet managed to add the coincidences in her life, but she suspected the irony of the sum: that she would find happiness when all she could recall were the least of her crimes. Often, she would wake in the middle of the night, discover herself sitting in the middle of her bed, the sheets flung off her body, her fingers retaining a dream-memory of fondling her mother's pink scalp, all fragile flesh except for a single strand of hair lying across the exposed area. The ridge of that thin hair would feel like a scar that simply refused to abate.

MY *SAISON* BETWEEN BAUDELAIRE AND MORRISON

I would have to find someone who would follow me in my wanderings.
— November 10, 1890 letter from Arthur Rimbaud to his mother

Rock and roll loves you. As do spies. There is a season for everything and you called yours *Hell*. But you would not have had it otherwise. You deconstructed rainbows—peeling apart each color to assign to vowels. Adolescents worldwide become arsonists mistaking your *Fire* for fire. (Instead of *Love*.) They sip absinthe, but know not when stupor is mere approximation: a lie.

I know why you became a businessman. I have worn that silk and wool. The ledgers categorize. Then they count. Those journals never fold from the ripple of a breeze, are never felled by the sight of a tiger butterfly. Such calmness can be convenient. As convenient as emptied waterfalls, the breaking mist relegated to pale text cringing its way across thin paper—only to be crumpled or blown away by the weakest breath. Then memory is forced to suffice, its dim hallways quivering from inebriation instead of responsibility: oh, that attempt at lucidity!

The blood still seeps through the darkened continent you left without succor. The blood still spills. A century later I must reconcile with your grandchildren. They never spill viscous tears. Nor do they satiate. But I lose myself in their indigent beds, lick the drawn shadows beneath their eyes, to goad your hand into mine. When another dawn arrives—persistent with the clarity of a sunlit day—again I make do with purple figs as a compromise.

Fold around me (I beg you). For you, I keep midnight company. For you, I look for lovers to send me red roses. I like to inhale their scent as I turn their bodies upside down. I hang them on flaccid doorknobs. Against the tarnished metal, the petals flutter before they stiffen, then die. Then they live forever in that consistently rapturous pose. That full bloom of it. Its unrelentingness. Its consistently rapturous bloom. Its unrelentingness

THE ELEVENTH WEDDING ANNIVERSARY

"From thee the madman and the leper learn to prize,
Through love, a most unlikely taste of Paradise"
— from "The Litanies of Satan" by Charles Baudelaire

The house is emptying. Among the shadows clinging to the corners of its rooms, dust curls like fists. Their clench lacks interruption—like air spilling undistracted onto newly-stark floors. She stands in the foyer, as silent as the reproach of the walls. Nails begin rusting in their holes. Then, there are holes, implacably widening. She begins to feel the flow within her veins rising towards crescendo. When she begins to weep, her heart also breaks at the inevitable shatter that must occur for this teardrop so compelling it persuades rainbows to cling to its quivering complexion while attempting suspension in mid-air.

He told her, *I concede I have lived too long without introspection.* His pose was awkward, but his spine stood as straight as an empty flagpole. She forced herself to face the springtime in his eyes. It was supposed to be a different season. But, as he conceded, there is a lapse with which he long ago forced resolution. *What if I waved our flag once more?* he asked unexpectedly. She thought she had finished her descent through purgatory until he, somehow, birthed that question. For she had forgotten how many stars are supposed to shine in that referenced flag. She has forgotten all about stars—those pricks that would widen to sunder night, to bring forth light.

Oh, how she detested their seventh year of marriage. The months were indeterminable as he tossed off a crowd-pleaser: *I told her not to bother about the seven-year itch. I tried it three years ago and found it no big deal.* Once more, the denuded walls unleashed laughter loosened by her husband's predictable wit during a Halloween affair. Everyone lurked behind face masks, except for her husband who, earlier that day, clasped gold over the pale skin throbbing with her panicked pulse. He never bothers to shield his eyes, while she liked the feathers against her face softly hiding everything but the wet gleam of her gaze. She was comforted by redundant camouflages.

She loves to wander empty streets at dawn. The boulevards are empty, and they are pink. Once, she saw another intruder quickly turn left rather than allow their walks to parallel. It was a monk in a blue robe. Or, was it a redhead in a black ballgown? No, it was a redhead in a blue robe. She must have lived in the neighborhood as she also carried a mug of steaming coffee (or perhaps tea?). Undoubtedly, she must be married and perhaps was escaping her kids, even temporarily. Sometimes, one simply must flee from what one loves the most. It is an important, though *dissonant,* note.

MUSE POEM

She spends her days in a dusty room, its lone window shuttered, the air lit with the glow from a computer screen, and stacks of books melting into the shadows. This is the way it should be. Her eyes are open to a parallel universe where silence is alien, for silence has no color. She sees no reason to censor the mountain from saffron, the sky from celadon, the boulder from lavender, the bougainvillea from cobalt, the grass from ebony, the diamond from cerise, or you from me.

Or me from you. But everything costs. To define the Muse as *forgetting memory* is to begin by birthing a mask, then becoming subservient to it. Even if one must learn to allow shackles on one's wrists, fall to one's knees—then bow once more after begging for more lashes from the whip. All for the hope that welts will be permanent to create new parts of my body that may rise at the thought of your touch.

The use of third-party pronouns in a poem will not spare me from the sight of your back receding as the door slowly closes. *This* is the way it should be. I must crawl towards where I recall the door to be, uncertain of who you have become on the other side. When I find the door by scenting blood, I must open it by first remembering fear. I must remember fear. For nothing must be silenced. There must be color.

Like the color of *Wet:* bittersweet, bloodshot, blooming, blush, brick, burgundy, cardinal, carmine, cerise, cherry, chestnut, claret, copper, coral, crimson, dahlia, flaming, florid, flushed, fuchsia, garnet, geranium, glowing, healthy, inflamed, infrared, magenta, maroon, pink, puce, rose, roseate, rosy, rubicund, ruby, ruddy, russet, rust, salmon, sanguine, scarlet, titian, vermilion, wine. . .

Nothing must be silenced. There must be color. Though I remember fear, I have heard the memory of a Taoist shaman whispering: "Bright pure color represents the virtue. Bright white for strength, courage and rectitude. Bright blue for gentleness and wisdom. Bright green for kindness and benevolence. Bright golden yellow for balance, centeredness and fairness. Bright red for love, joy and compassion." I must remember fear, before remembering to forgive myself.

Nothing must be silenced. There must be color. Like the color of *Wet.* RED.

THE LAMB

She mourns his departure though he has yet to turn towards the door. He even tries to check her grief with a paltry joke. But both realize she is compelled by self-defense. So she must continue, and he must not object. She must continue her tears. They fall like a reluctant daylight.

Once, he tried for permanence and asked her to tea. Though she consistently attempts to solidify the memory of their communion by recalling how the air turned as florid as mint concentrate lingering on her tongue, he never repeated the occasion of "welcomed conflagration." One evening, after he cast away the world by shutting the door into his destitute studio, he walked towards a mirror. His face relaxed into an unsmiling gravity. His face relaxed, though he shook his head at recognizing the million slivers that comprised the reflection.

She knows he is trapped by his selfishness. He believes it too late to change direction, except perhaps to marry an heiress who would be generous without demands. He would not mind an English butler. It would facilitate listening to Puccini without worrying about the finity of time. He envisions himself in a book-lined room, his feet lifted atop a damask-covered ottoman as his fingers waltzed to notes weighting the air. Perhaps a high note would evoke regret, but he would survive that. Perhaps a high note would evoke *her*, and he would survive that, too. And if ever an heiress pops her innocent face through the 16th century mahogany doorway, her face would be as blurred as his sight is clear on what is entailed by sacrifice.

TAUROMACHIA

What she hides from her father is how she prefers her particular difficulty to the legacy he wishes to provide. But how to say *that* when she knows his legacy is the only chance he has at ascribing value to his life? (Mother cannot help.) What one must do . . .

He loves to tell her this story: she is two years old, clad in a white dress with ribbons threaded through her hair. Lace edges her pink socks. She is propped on his knee as they sit beneath a star-apple tree. They rub noses, rub-a-dub-dub, as she gurgles with glee. Her chubby fists clutch at his fingers as if she'll never let go. Ever. Orchids unfurl to show yellow stamen. Ants are left alone.

But if I was not born innocent does it matter? Place a finger in the midst of my palm. Feel the pulse where my lifeline ends. The pulse there is a gypsy's flamenco. My dress is cut from violet leather. Underneath, thin slivers of fuschia silk. And a green tattoo of a thorn to discover only when intimacy is unmitigated. You want to join me, don't you, as I hunt myself?

But, mother has come to worship Kali

MUSTERING

"Then I would know if standing beside you leaves my lips dry."
— **from "Thinkable Pictures" by Rosmarie Waldrop**

It need not take more than one person to bring the world to ruin. One woman with a face so lovely it inspires a fleet of warships musters what it takes. As does one man, impoverished in spirit but holding the key to a black box with a lever that, pulled down, shatters a satellite in space. The blast would repel meteors that formerly wove a camouflage

and shift openings on desert surfaces back on earth. Long, black guns would rise from its depths to loosen the heat of a nuclear winter on unsuspecting civilians riding camels on different continents. (And the animals, too, would contain entreaty in their brown, intelligent eyes.) Perhaps the civilians' only crimes would have been to mistake ignorance for anonymity. *No one is anonymous in this world.* I once told an honorable man before he sealed his scars and left me: by his act,

for as long as he musters a life-prolonging breath, there will be a matching exhale by one who considers him with enmity, "always." No doubt, I would lift that spell off his countenance if I knew today where he walks his shadows, where he bows his face. There would be white blooms on cherry trees and kindness in my gaze. But perhaps I am the court jester, complete with polka-dotted outfits that hurt the sight

in the court of those Born Again renewing their faith. A woman with a straight back has bound her thick hair in generous ribbons of burgundy damask. She is reclaiming the throne. "The King is dead! Long live us all!" And the gold scepter is light in her roughened hand. And her gown cheerfully displaces air, fullsome with silk layers and silver thread. And long, yellow banners float out of the windows to skim the air over cheering crowds. But there is always someone whose presence we glean only through his shoes peering from beneath the drapes of velvet walls. It is always a cruel man. Is he Chief of Staff? Or is he the power behind? I do not need to see his mask to exercise control over what my eyes wish to do. I first met him in the front line of a personal revolution. Afterwards, when I face a mirror, my eyes—

they wish to fall,

     they wish to stall.

AMBER

*And he asked: Where is this Tambobo again that the sand in your
shoes came from? And he said it was spitting distance from Borneo,
and lay somewhere below the stairway to heaven.*
— Alfred Yuson

She felt the Mindanao Sea salt her breasts and realized: she long
has wished to drop out from the world. Once, a saint counseled,
"Faith is the substance of things hoped for and the evidence of
things not seen." She began to consider the thatched hut by the
beach that tempted her to linger for a night. The simple structure
lacked walls and no matter which direction she faced she
blossomed from feeling the sky's embrace. She began to consider
remaining by this wave-less shore that offered an emotion she
welcomed as a discovery: *suspension.*

Beyond the hut, the ground rose to hide the path she walked to
reach the beach. The slope hid the flame trees that dropped
rubicund blossoms along her cheeks when she tilted her face
towards a bird's cry. She welcomed their perfume that she knew
she would sense with every sunset beginning the dark hours of
rumination. As sleep can never be foretold or controlled, she
persistently searched for any source of color to light her dreams.
She believed a sunlit sensibility to be an admirable goal.

Nevertheless, she always grappled with a desire for death. For
death attempts a seduction whenever she "eroticizes history" to
transcend the past? An Irish poet once replied to her dilemma,
she should revise the word "death" with the word "birth." The
poet held her hand as the poet explained: "the same sensibility, a
different form." Though she remained loyal to her native form,
she agreed with the poet, which is why she longed to become the
fossilized secret within the immoveable embrace of gold. *This*
would be "suspension" lit by a flame: a beauty unable to lose its
luster despite the unrelenting advent of karma.

RESPECT

I am beginning to count the bricks that form the building across Broadway. This is why you fail to appreciate my addiction to opium. The sun prepares its bed, transforming bricks from grey to the color of your cheeks ruddy in a winter chill. I feel apples begin to fall in orchards upstate. Soon, vinegar will scent the air and it will be a discordant note that will please.

And the rain continues so! I long for bystanders to release the broken roof formed by umbrellas whose broken spines they begrudge. (How long, after all, must servitude be forced?) The lone umbrella bobbing obstinately against the storm is stamped with a corporate logo: a snake swallowing its tail. But I am succeeding in "looking between raindrops" until I feel the impatient drumming of your fingers on the window ledge.

You also disappointed me in Portugal. The bar boasted 500 different bottles of port. Consistency prevailed when what was offered differed from the advertisement. But you forced me to stay because you thought the "atmosphere like Eluard's street—a wound that will not close." I faced no choice but to indenture my gaze to your fascination with a fur-clad dancer. Her lips were painted crimson but I was bothered most by her hair which she wore up and threaded through with thin, black ribbons. My throat was elegantly white, its throbbing vein elegantly blue, but how to compete?

This is where fragmented syntax fails to suffice. I, too, might as well die by moaning through the *fado*. That, or be an old man huddled in a confidence with the bartender as we watch a new woman accompany a guitar. Afterwards, she would join us, slowly descending from the make-shift stage, her ample hips swaying, her eyes looking only sideways, her breasts robust and proudly raised. Still, we would greet her with respect: our eyebrows never would rise, never would suspect.

LATIN

The necklace of rubies was an introduction. He thought to
surprise her with a proposition. But she replied, *I have never liked
my men on their knees!* He mustered a stand, blinking at the sun
rays striking the gems she was inspecting. Finally, she said, *I
prefer my stones harder.* But he knew as he walked away, forlorn,
that had he given her diamonds there still would have been no
guarantees. Worst, he could feel her gaze on his back and it lacked
enmity.

In his absence, she reached for a decanter and stained a crystal
glass into amber. For a pensive moment, she held the crystal
towards the generous light from a brass chandelier. She thought
once more of her hidden desire: to freeze time around her, even if
she must become a poor creature trapped in a honey-colored
casket. For she has trained men to kneel and she is replete. *Fit in
dominata servitus. In servitude dominatus.* But she coughed over
her first swallow and recoiled at being surprised.

Then she reared at her reflection in the mirror. A stain was
spreading across her shoulder. She reached for it and her
uncontrolled gesture elongated its darkness across white, raw silk.
The fabric wrapped around her breasts began to feel less than the
price she paid for it. She had reached for it in SoHo's chicest
boutique where she was waited on by a slim, tall man fearlessly
dangling a thin mustache. The glimmer had compelled a memory
of a lightning bolt cracking a summer night over Abiqui, New
Mexico. She had reached for it and been surprised when her
fingers touched something tangible that she thought was a bright
light. And as the Kentucky whiskey continued to torture the silk,
she began to consider whether she should attempt something else.
Perhaps sweetness

THE FAIRY CHILD'S PRAYER

— for Rene "Master Dragon" Navarro and painter Max Gimblett

Because the sky can never be a margin against my desire, I raise my hand to you and, in so doing, compel the swoop of the falcon with jade eyes, cobalt breast and ebony feathers. I have emptied my bag of tricks, released the barbed wire from its tattooed bracelet about my left wrist. The shade recedes as I refuse to look away from interpretations overwrought but opaque. I shall learn Faith by keeping my eyes on the sun until a life's definition becomes a synonym for the sky's cerulean gift: an attic door to face without trepidation. Those who ascended after their initial falls now frolic with stars swirling in the *cosmic microwave background*—obviating directions like "top" or "bottom" as the world is more than a diamond: its glory includes facets marred by trapped flecks of coal. You said of Life: "It is all stunning— including the shadow." The Milky Way that grazes the Maori mountains of your birthland is the same silvery cascade that threads through my hair as my mind's eye wanders through a universe I once thought I inherited instead of something I can help paint. You nudge my memory for afternoons of pollination: lemon dust attaching to the centers of open flowers whose petals form light's prism. The sky, you teach me, shall never drop. For in a distant past, I loved well enough to earn wings formed with gold wire, not wax: soon, I shall soar. My tongue shall yet become a bolt of white velvet I shall swathe around our planet and hold as an infant against my milk-laden breasts. When the horizon stuns again, it shall be from the *sumi* ink you brushed against dawn's canvas, evoking my hands when, for the first time, they shall be graceful as they dance the new and ancient form: "Fairy Child Praying to the Goddess of Mercy Kuanyin Shaoling Kung-Fu Fist."

MY STATEN ISLAND FERRY POEM

To be taken up higher and higher by uneven stone stairs and to stand
there with your heart beating outside the gate of the near world. To
gather laurel and marble for the white architecture of your destiny.
And to be as you were born, the center of the world.
— **Odysseus Elytis**

You tell me the lights remind you of Tuscany, the fires in homes
dotting the hillsides. I am looking at these same stars and see
dying men in white shirts toiling past midnight in the skyscrapers
of Manhattan. Beneath our feet, the Hudson is gentle for once,
like the cheek of a woman's face in repose. Are you looking at me
as I tilt my face elsewhere to hide the yearning in my gaze? A
cloud lifts and the pale moon is unclothed. Then its silver shadow
ripples across the water, loosening languid drops of mercury.
Translucent pearls warm my skin. I hear flint struck on the other
side of our earth: gasp with delight as its heat burns white against
my eyes.

I often amuse you with my fantasies of other men you know
better than I do. These are the poets in Manila who feel I am only
five years old—they tape all my watercolors against their windows
so that sun rays enter their homes as rainbows. And you? You
merely keep loosening the generous ball of twine from which I
soar: a kite in flight, dangling but which you never let fall. I might
be a dragon, a raven, a butterfly or Glinda riding her broom. Or I
might be a salvaged piece of pockmarked paper, its edges glued
around sticks to approximate some shape of geometry. Always,
you never enforce gravity, though we know it is a temptation you
ignore.

Later, our friend Curtis will cackle about this all-night ride on the
Staten Island Ferry. "Boy, you'd think you all were in high school
or something!" he will tease. I remember when I was that young.
I possessed more hair and they fell to the back of my knees. I
wore platform shoes with seven-inch heels. *Dittos* was THE

brand of jeans—I wore them in saffron shades of orange to befit
the California sunshine. I had a waist (oh, those 24 inches!) that
my low-slung *Dittos* and abbreviated blouses revealed. An ocean
away, in a city I know today as Manila, you were chasing Rimbaud
and smoking. We would have hated each other back then. It is no
longer *back then*.

The stairs are uneven and I cannot see where they halt their rise. I
climb, pause for air by inhaling whole whirlwinds, then climb once
more. Still, the stone ledges do not reveal their climax—is it a
"happily ever after" or a cruel joke's punch line? I climb and
climb until the rush of water is turbulent in my ears. It is like
what I am hearing with you tonight on the Staten Island Ferry.
The river is lyrical with its minute swells. The clouds are so far
away. The moon is content. And all I hear as the fires burn in
Tuscany straight ahead is the rush of memories yet to be birthed.
The dock approaches. I peer through the darkness and latch onto
another breeze to soar. Straight ahead is a sunlit day, the press of
the sky against the horizon as careful as you. Consequently, the
horizon is invisible, masking where journeys are thought to end.

THE DESTINY OF RAIN

—after "Three Poems," ink on rice paper, by Eric Gamalinda

His friends missed him for months. When a season changed the light from winter silver to spring gold, he reappeared. His friends were not surprised with only one painting by his side to explain his prolonged absence. He said the painting required a process that was impossible to shortcut. His friends were silent as their eyes traced a single brushstroke against a panel of rice paper. The black paint rose until it thinned to a strand of white smoke. His friends were not surprised to smell the smoke, invisible against the white background. The scent was jasmine. His friends agreed with the title: *Innocence.*

He likes to point at solid objects that he can describe as "lucid." His friends have heard him say, *When a physical manifestation captures intent, it deserves appreciation.* In this category, he honors such lucid objects as the feather, the diamond, the rainbow, the rose, the apple, the bear and, especially, the air. His friends have seen him cup his palm, a gesture that made them feel, too, the weight there that he sees. Once, he looked at his friends and asked, *Negate night with me?* His loyal friends laughed at the weakness he displayed by expressing desire. But his friends understood: he was using speech to embody *Love.*

All friends have been hurt by the mirrors in his eyes. He leaves them dangling after he "takes their breath away." His friends know he is attempting to embody smoke. Inevitably, he will whiten into the clouds. His friends mock each other as they point at the sky for as long as spring lasts. By embodying seamlessness, the blue avoids imperfection: for him, storms are always in season. But, once, he mentioned *Love* and, for his friends, the compulsion in that act paid for an eternity of *Forgiveness.* His friends happily reconcile themselves to the destiny of rain.

THE CONTROLLING AGENT

The little boy squats so he can mimic an old man. A bird samples his bared knee before perching on his shoulder. Behind them a sun sets and the wind stops gasping. Palm trees sway in the dusk, floating from behind a pale river that ripple over cracked, ochre pebbles. Perhaps something lurks in the river grass, perhaps not.

She picks up the ancient carved figurine of the boy perched atop a piece of bamboo. Around the bamboo, a frieze of a river scene winds itself. Her finger traces the boy's tiny but plump cheeks, then the bird on his shoulder. She notices the bird has lifted one wing, as if about to fly away. She had thought this carven thing could be a toy for her nephew, but upon closer inspection she foretells accurately it would be a source of nightmare.

Yet, she takes it, dropping virgin bills in the wizened shopkeeper's palm. The old man barks briefly at her choice, then turns away to clear her throat, or pretend to do so. She likes to collect ghosts, you see, for the illusion she owns the years she knows she still must peel through. Increasingly, she has become afflicted with feelings of uncertainty about what lies beyond the perimeter of her sight.

Like, who had the ability long ago to look at a boy playing by a passive (was it not passive?) river and recognize a bird about to take flight? Oh, my love: who is subject and who is observer? What if the bird was perfectly content to stay with the boy? What if the observer is the controlling agent?

THE RECEPTIONIST

She cooks a chicken under unhappy circumstances as sirens rear beneath her window. She nods and concedes to men noisily rushing past her door: *Another sinner dies tonight.* She gnaws her lower lip until it bleeds. Still, the chicken percolates a homey, golden broth: she could be entrenched in corn fields, stalks waving blonde hair in a polite (Midwestern) breeze.

How she envied a waitress last night! She wore open-toed sandals crafted from snakeskin dyed orange. Her toes were as pink as the bellies of seashells littering her otherwise forlorn bureau. Once, a man wrote to *Cosmopolitan* magazine about "the cleavage of toes"—the sheer erotic flair of it! She ruminates with the memory, only to recall a teenage prostitute in Tijuana. It was the girl's day off and she wore an Easter bonnet cascading white lace. Despite church, her dress was too short as she would not concede by avoiding a display of chocolate limbs. In turn, she empathizes to feel a pew's worn velvet pressing like silk against scarred knees while the girl mustered a prayer for a priest-in-hiding.

And it is November, aghast as always with the bellows of wind. For weeks, she has not seen the sky become lurid. The absence of radioactivity births a desire to perm her thin hair. Otherwise she will maintain Sunday afternoons for large pots of chicken soup that inevitably go to waste. Hers is that of a single-person household, and she chooses friends among those alarmed by buildings lacking elevators. Still, she lives in an old building where ceilings were built high. Whenever she looks up at a dead light bulb she cannot reach to replace, she feels the walls giggling, then asking: *Where are the giants who once walked the earth?* Lately, she feels the walls have begun to sob the question. Sometimes, they do not question—merely sob.

Look: the cracks are widening! The mirrors are pressed against the walls! She cannot distinguish between her bloodshot eyes and the histrionically bawling walls! Yet only a receptionist's desk can end her Sundays.

IMMEDIATELY BEFORE

Winter proceeds on its own pace. She feels winter can never be too long. The lonely eye never fails to be pleased by floating snow. How it clings stubbornly to the impassive surface of glass skyscrapers!

She is not without experience. Once, she watched the spill of air in the rain forests of Brazil. For weeks, she watched air fall between the separation of branches, the quivering of leaves, atop immeasurably tall trees. She marveled then, *I can never tire of looking up*. She felt herself become an ancient statue of a warrior on horseback, fists raised while indomitably looking straight ahead.

Intention never suffices. But it is not without merit. She scolds herself, *Be nice. Be nice. He will be a kind lover. He will be a generous provider*. Then she collects herself at hearing how she has misapprehended her tenses. She already has made that decision that opened an interior closet to a Russian sable coat. The fur maintains the color and feel of heated butter, just before a total meltdown.

She forces herself to leave the poem. It is the moment she is accosted by two strangers at a neighboring table in a stereotyped cafe. It is a man's hand reaching to stroke a woman's cheek. It is a woman's cheek reaching to meet the tips of a man's fingers. Subsequently, the man pulls the woman's chair closer to his knees. Both are smiling. She also senses that both are awed: that each awes the other. The woman has hair like the Russian sable she rarely wears: the color of heated butter, just before a total meltdown. That immediately before

THE CASE FOR APLOMB

Truth insists. Dusk recalls ancient women unbinding combs discreetly seeded with pearls. Somewhere in the bowels of SoHo, a nude clenches eyes to paint a floor magenta with glistening hair. Witnesses comprise cruel men in Wall Street suits and Greenwich, Connecticut wives. Still, the sun will greet a new day with equal opportunity.

Once, a young girl approached me as my tears dampened a street corner in London. The sheen on her cheeks belied ulterior motives. She offered a fist so that, she whispered, she could unclench it for me. The air her palm unmasked was generous and fondled me with the cheer of undiluted innocence.

I would like to fall in love one day with a policeman. S/he need not be American. No continent can contain my fidelity. Only the boozy notes finishing the moans of sweating women. They are usually overweight, these earnest women able to flit with fortitude between sequined dresses and church choir gowns. Their capacities heighten my hunger and I long to unite the convex with the concave

FRANZ KLINE KINDLY SAYS ABOUT THREE GESTURE-LADEN BRUSHSTROKES

He considers two fields in warring countries whose politicians are experts in barter. He believes these two fields to share a symbiotic relationship. One has been contaminated by industrial waste. While one is abundant with *Brassica napus, Thiaspi alpestre* and *Festuca rubra*—plants known as hyperaccumulators for leeching off metal contaminants from earth. I consider his concerns and long for the giant sunflowers of Munich. When they blocked the sun, I treasured the solicitousness of their shade. When I bowed in gratitude, my gaze attached itself to sprays of tiny, pink roses threaded through a white lattice fence. Such is the measure of "replete"! How he tempts me to succumb!

Allow the heart its complete measure of each decision, then of each act including the flux of a prior motivation. Allow the mind the implication of the *kundiman*, a love song that bears roots in a military ballad. One is mostly seduced by uncertainty. Is not war but another exercise in risk-management? He kept pushing and pushing, but did not anticipate she would transcend a fall by consciously dashing into a dive from the highest point of an edge. As she fell, she looked behind her at the dark silhouette of a man frozen against a sunlit sky. He refused to follow her. She transferred her eyes towards what her act deemed inevitable— chose to replace bitterness with a lucid observation of the dangers awaiting her. After all, he once suggested, "Blow up the world if you must. But avoid ambiguity."

He married a woman to reward her for chasing him. What does it mean that he didn't leave her after I subsequently chased him? Yet on their wedding night, he called me from a phone booth a few feet away from the entrance to a hotel that mimicked a cake with *ma-drama* frosting one may kindly call "baroque." There is something to be said for the lack of responsibility associated with transforming oxygen into a branch weighted with leaves of such generosity that each leaf is as wide and as widening as an oil spill. It is foolish to envy the snake swallowing its tail simply because a circle denotes perfection. That "something to be said" is to recognize *some days should begin elsewhere.* Although, that "something (that should) be said" is also not: NO.

ABANDONING MISERY

"dissonance may abandon *miserere*"
— *from "Dissonance Royal Traveller" by Barbara Guest*

She considers the monarch butterfly predictable: the flit of those
wings, but then to alight on the sweetest bud swaying with a
random, forlorn breeze. It could be the hot breath of summer:
always returning, lapsed into a rut. Beyond the horizon, a
mountain peaks, a nimbus separates, a cock buries its red tufted
head—but to follow the arc of a circle will find the sun rising
somewhere, the sky blazing a red carpet for its ascent. It may even
be the sky over Burkina Faso.

"All ages are impressionable," an old poet once said. Another
said, "I wanted passion—I got it, and its punishment, too. . . . I
got all the violence that accompanies desire." She had hoped to
leave matters there. But a third poet unexpectedly revealed, "I
avoid the touch of money; I believe it will curse me into the next
life." In response, she closed her eyes to remember the
shimmering air over a datsan in Siberia: three taps, a wheel turns,
she prays—searching for the smile behind a Buddha's impassive
face.

In another time, she wore white dresses: hems concluding with
satin ribbons. She wore bows in her hair, dimples in her cheeks, a
charm bracelet around her wrist and a gold locket dangling over
her prideful chest. She loved (loves) her mother, adored (adores)
her father—and as she, years later, considers their mortality she
begins to sing lullabys. Her songs bring her parents to ballrooms
blazing with light from chandeliers overhead, generous sconces on
the walls, the gleam of crystal, the reflection from gold-edged
mirrors, the sheen on the band's brass instruments and, finally, the
love in her own eyes. When men loosen their chains to dive off
ships for her songs, or when she bares her heart to the unflinching
spears of jagged rocks, stolid against the ocean's waves, she feels,
There simply is no need to apologize.

INSOMNIA'S LULLABYE

— for Jose Ayala, Michelle Bautista and Barbara Reyes

I keep tearing off slips from the sky so I can peel off the stars like children's candy on wax paper. Tonight, the stars are flavored strawberry—sufficient to make me recall a birthday party that ended with real strawberries dipped into something white and gooey (though I can't recall: was the sauce vanilla ice cream, melted marshmallows or steamed milk?). Now, my fingers are stained with the sweet juice of a color associated with (com)passion and still—oh, still!—I tear slips from the sky.

I have wondered what the sky hides. I now tell you that the sky camouflages the destiny of forgotten memories. The last piece of torn sky, for one, revealed the pursed lips of a tall man to whom I once whispered, "I hear your voice all the time and it's been years since you've said anything new to me."

Tear the sky and you discover it bleeds as you once bled when I shook your hands from my shoulders as you attempted to console me. What I didn't concede then was that I was bleeding, too, as I felt the weight of your touch evaporate into the dusk graying the light. None were consoled when I added, "This isn't happening. This, too, shall be cloaked by a dispassionate sky."

Have I even mentioned yet the frigorific blast of wind blowing across the midnight-purple surface of the lake?

I tear off another strip and realize, soon, I shall sleep. For I have achieved what I did not know was my goal when my hands started clawing at night's ceiling. I have brought back the memory of three friends who reminded me that flowers bear their own names. Poets know that naming is identity-making. As the trio of happy faces fall from their atmospheric cubicles to which they were consigned by my amnesia, my eyelids begin to droop.

Tonight, the stars circle my *pusod* like a miniature Milky Way.

Tonight, I remember and recover Michelle, Barbara and Joey
feeding me *balut, sinigang* soup, white rice and *longanisa*.
Afterwards, I won't even faint from scouring a huge pot so that I
can join in their banter. All this was foretold centuries ago by a
haruspex but since he remains quivering now behind the night sky,
I had to experience and cure insomnia to remember how
moonlight on Fifth Street silvered everything it touched—

       like the wind chime and the four poets it delighted with its
song.

RAPUNZEL, ENRAPT

*"stairs rising to platforms lower than themselves,
doors leading outside that bring you back inside"*
— ***Clifford Geertz, on Michel Foucault***

She locks the entrance to the turret containing a thousand diaries
whose papers are yellowed and leather covers cracked. Then she
feeds the key to an alligator. She is outside where ants clamber up
the velvet folds masking her thighs (she actually scents grass!).
She understands gloves are old-fashioned but has resigned herself
to certain constraints: it takes time for the ink stains on her hands
to fade. But she has crossed the moat. As she peers at the stolid,
grey tower that she once draped with her hair, that a man once
climbed, she shivers but smiles.

First, she must eliminate her guides. Her godfather—an emperor
of two continents and the eagles overhead—has sent a troop of
retired generals. She can feel their white beards swaying as they
urge black stallions toward her. She can hear the horses gasp as
effort glazes a wet sheen over their hides. Though the shimmer of
air in the distance simply may be the temper of a summer day, she
lifts her skirts and breaks forth into a run.

Once, a man buried his face into her shaking hands. She treasured
the alien rush of warmth against her fingers as he spoke of sand,
gritty but fine; of waves, liquid yet hard; of ships, finite spaces but
treasured for what they may explore; of ocean breezes, invisible
but salty on the tongue. "Like the potential for grief?" she asked.
He raised his eyes in surprise and she captured his gaze. She
pressed on, "I have read that grief is inevitable with joy." Still, she
woke one day to a harsh rope dangling from an opened window,
and emptiness was infinite by her side.

Now, she is taking the path opposite from the direction she saw
the man choose when he departed. As his hands left the rope, he
looked up and saw her lack of bitterness framed in the window.

The forest respected her grief with a matching silence. But she had learned from the Egyptians how to measure intangible light, a lesson that revealed the earth to curve. Now, she runs and as she begins to gasp, she can feel the sand between her toes, the breezes tangle the long strands of her hair and the waves weight her skirts. And as she begins to feel his ship disrupting the horizon, a sheen breaks across her brow and she feels her lips part. Enrapt, she knows she soon will take off her gloves. Enrapt, she feels she is getting there

AGAINST DISAPPEARANCE

> *"A stake, an axis is thus driven into the earth in order to mark out the boundaries of the sacred space in many patriarchal traditions. It defines a meeting place for men that is based upon an immolation. Women will in the end be allowed to enter that space, provided that they do so as nonparticipants."*
> — **Luce Irigaray**

After she climbed down the tower, Rapunzel looked at the welts rising on her palms. She had not expected the burn inflicted by the braided rope. Still, she allowed her tears to water the red tracks that began her new journey. For she had learned that bliss is possible only to those who first experience pain. As the salt of her tears stoked the fire in her grasp, she pronounced to the doves she felt lurking among the high branches of surrounding trees: *One must fly toward the space where the distance towards the horizon can never be measured.*

Once, a man dodged the floating spotlights of her guards to climb towards the window of the turret where she spent her days in velvet gowns, living through words she read behind covers of cracked leather. She was surprised as she had not thrown down her hair which remained pinned under her inheritance of gold combs festooned with diamonds, rubies, emeralds and pearls. "Don't move," he ordered as he walked towards her. "I want to memorize the way you look, before your hair will fall from the pleasure I will teach you." And as the sun's departure stained the sky beyond her window, her hair fell. And her lips parted. And her gown slipped down her shoulders to reveal the silk and lace woven by those who once served her ancestors whose portraits adorned her walls. She looked at her father and nodded slightly to acknowledge the foretelling of a frown the artist had painted on his brow. But her hands rose to grasp the man tighter against her breasts as she whispered: *Before the first one, how does one know sin?*

The shadow of a dove in flight interrupted her reverie. Her tears ceased and she wiped her palms against the velvet covering her thighs. Then she lifted her skirts and danced down a gravel path whose unknown destiny she did not mind. She danced with a swath of silver butterflies who appeared from nowhere and lingered over her smile. Until an old male dwarf from another fairy tale popped his head from behind a boulder by the bend of the path and asked, "Who are you?" She proclaimed with glee and pride, "I am Rapunzel." To which the dwarf replied, "Nonsense: Rapunzel has long hair!" And she laughed and announced as she twirled in a circle so that her skirts flared high to reveal the lack of silk hose against her bare legs, "I cut my hair, braided it into a rope, and used it to escape my turret!" Amazed, the dwarf said, "How did you think of that unusual idea?" Rapunzel stopped her dance, fixed a cold stare at the dwarf and hissed like Clytemnestra: *When women control their destinies, they are only exercising a law of nature. How dare you be surprised!*

RETURNING THE BORROWED TONGUE

warm stones gather the rainfall
speaking a gray language
i've tried to imitate.
i read books compiled
from anonymous scrolls.
i eat their dust
hoping to trace
the steps to heaven.
      — from ": Looking For Buddha" by Jaime Jacinto

He cannot seem to stop trading one ocean for another. Back and forth, he rides different waves. One day, a gentle wave with warm surf depositing him by a green and orange fisherman's boat, overhead a sunlit sky. Another day, a squall pounding against the face of an implacable cliff, no sun in sight—and he is clinging to a slippery boulder, shivering. Either way, he cannot sleep in a room whose window does not overlook water. He notes, *I am my own bridge.*

Once, she dropped out of the world by joining a caravan of students traversing Siberia towards Lake Baikal. It was November and the River Angara that fed the lake had thawed into shifting pieces of grey slate. But the lake remained frozen, like the endless bank of clouds she had stared at from her airplane's window. A stranger had clutched at her arm, whispering, "I am inexplicably afraid our plane will drop." The lack of fear in her eyes over this possibility provided no relief, she knew, but it was the best she could offer for consoling a stranger's premonition about life. The stranger's fear evoked Lucifer. But she did not question why she held a false memory of witnessing this angel's fall.

He asked her to accompany him on one of his transitions towards the direction of a country whose people can never control their arms from enfolding invaders against their hearts. She replied with sorrow, *I can be myself only in exile.* He did not look back as he departed for an ocean whose salt he already could taste, whose embrace he already could savor against his naked back and whose sun he already could kiss with his uplifted face. Both knew she will wait on the other side of the earth that he must continue circling until he is felled to his knees. And, when on his knees, he still will continue moving forward, she will be the altar that will halt his travel, make him stand, then stay.

For this fable, there are no words. There only is the *Breaking (of) Silence:* the evenings of solitary grace in a dim room, at a desk a piece of blank paper spotlit by the beam of a lone lamp and, yes, one more attempt with the wake of yet another day.

TRIPTYCH FOR ANNE TRUITT

only raid the world of
its radiance and wonder
—from "Cezanne's Apples" by Manuel Viray

BEGINNING LUCIDITY

— after DAYBOOK THE JOURNAL OF AN ARTIST
by Anne Truitt

Is the most difficult lesson one of submission: a spine bent
willingly for a stranger's whip? How to reach something when we
wake to find ourselves clutching the wet manes of panicked
horses? And the only certainty about what lies beyond the drop of
a path riddled with dangerous gravel is that there, too, "unanimous
night" remains? I am trying this ride one can only make alone—
that choking run towards a moment of light within the cloak of
ragged breathing.

Sometimes, only erasures capture the threshold of consciousness.
Why am I always drawn to the imperceptible? Why is there
precedent for this curiosity by women marking time from the first
farewell of a man? *Noli me tangere*—and still one feels it all,
though the drain of emotion is persistently inevitable. One must
pay the price of living on the spine to be a vessel for
enlightenment. Is there consolation in this potential even as one
begins to pace on the edges of knives? Do I really want to know
why a permanent wound can be cut by a certain look from a child?

What kind of existence do we force on our days when we wish
pain to remain unmitigated? Is that like poets laying pen against
paper to approximate worlds without physicality? Is that like one
more artist painting white on white on white? Perhaps I am
forgetting that "faith" is religion without words, without buildings
whose roofs block the sky. Indeed, sages welcome honey for its
texture: a stubborn clinging fashioned from the sheen of precious
metals. And I have heard angels from the Milky Way whisper
through the fall of stars: "Jasmine is the scent of gold."

We teach our children that conversation can be a thin blanket for

pain. But even a boor pauses before a Rembrandt self-portrait. I
love a man who praises Rembrandt for painting his humanity
beyond reprieve. But this man also repelled my child and now he
thinks of thresholds solely for capturing shadows caused by a
son's return. I love a man who looks at the world through a glass
of heartbreaking resignation. What does this say about me?

Perhaps I am attempting to use color to prevent encounters from
degenerating into lies? Afterthoughts always muster the musk of
long-locked rooms—the musk of grey. I would like to believe I
prefer what are held in common by rainbows and sapphires. I
would rather continue down the path towards larger definitions.
This, too, is why I believe criticizing artists is a waste of time, even
if critics have glossy paper at their disposal. Character
underwrites us all.

And what joy to recognize the curved line as both convex and
concave—a moment close to my backbone. We should praise
Greek poets for not bothering to alleviate heartbreak, but in
addressing it only for fueling aspiration. Yet Plato shows me how
I long to follow Prometheus—how deeply I feel the need to dance
with vultures under a menopausal sun. I want, I want . . . to be
wrung, to be rung!

Yes, I am intrigued by how we take the straight line for granted.
Unless we have felt money diminish like the draining of marrow.
Once, I saw a purple orchid with a pink stamen. I was shopping
for a used car, but noticed through peripheral vision the flower on
a crumbling windowsill. Now I appreciate rust. From this same
process, I have chosen to become more feminine in behavior. I
believe this means I am now a bat who operates through radar.

How to be as plain as bread chewed by oenophiles to clear their
palates? I want to live in those moments when energy starts to

become visible through physical effect. Like a poor girl from my childhood who wore a dress I outgrew. Everyday for three months, silk lace fondled a neck that increasingly thinned until I could count the ropes stretched along her throat. They evoked the sounds of hot days: ice rattling in pitchers of spent lemons as sugar fails against insistent sourness.

Apparently, the back of my hair is marked by a stranger's crimson paint. As it is January, I must have brushed against a building's attempt to greet a new year. I was trying to overcome the holidays by meandering down Main Street. I always compliment January for leaving light as plain as it could be. I like the courage of women who refuse to paint their lips. They are not like me, who love to stain whatever I kiss. I like to kiss because, too often, murder can occur simply through the seamless pass by an eye. I like to kiss because all of life is precious and "fragile." All of life is fragile.

Oh, how often I ask myself: "What did I know? What do I know?" Is it enough to find joy in a sunray slipping past the shutters to allow dust motes their tango? What suffices when I have seen bliss deep within the eyes of an ascetic who wanders the world with a beggar's bowl? What can I truly hope for when, sometimes, all decisions are made by color? Once, I drove through a forest in New Hampshire and saw a painting by Cezanne as I made a left turn. But, so quickly did I leave it behind—this eye's inadvertent slip that forever marks me like a heart tattoo against an inner thigh.

Some wounds never heal. With age, she has learned to avoid pricking at them. But, occasionally, her foot slips and, once more — and I become tired as I note this to you—once more, she plunges. When all of my hair turned white, my reflection noted, "Down is faster than up." Matter is so stubborn that even Art can become about coping with the physical. Even your refusal to bear progeny fails to silence my pleas for shackled wrists. Or, how I long for your blindfold so I can beg, "Please: bare my breasts. Please: I want to feed your pleasure." Then once more: "Please."

I don't believe death is the final tenderness for death confirms the wisdom of choices that seek to exalt solitude. I overheard an old lady tell her companion: "One of the unexpected delights of parenthood is the reversal of being put to bed by a child." I have asked many among you whether I am naive to believe love need not be solipsistic. The man I love replied, No. So I have come this far to discover the beauty within a cloud chamber: the traces of intersecting trajectories. For the man I love quoted Emerson as he held me tight: "The health of the eye always demands a horizon. We are never tired so long as we can see far enough." I believe the man I love was telling me: "Do not fear the distance between physical objects. Learn how detachment includes."

ILLUSIONS THROUGH THE GRID

— *after* TURN THE JOURNEY OF AN ARTIST *by Anne Truitt*

A white rattlesnake has invaded my dreams. Its body slithered into
my world, blissfully ignorant that its presence will not be benign.
A pale snake, almost luminescent in its youth, suffices to create a
revelation: through marriage, I have harbored self-delusion, as if
by nestling onto my husband's chest each night I delivered unto
him a set of dangerous experiences that I will never have to learn.
For his diamonds protect me. But I should know better by my
consistent ability to ask certain questions: like, why need "dusk"
define itself by light leaving the sky?

Artemisia looks beyond the tremulous cliff and feels the tug of a
void's unrelenting gravity. The court painter responds, "Map space
into a grid. Then look through each square. What do you see?"
She licks her lips before whispering, "Unrequited love. Unrequited
life." Well-fed, he is looking through the same piece of intuitive
square but sees only a wisp of white flickering in and out of
visibility. "Perhaps it is a stray piece of a cloud," he suggests to
comfort her. Because she is a virgin, Artemisia blocks from her
mind the colors of a scream: the regret of crimson, the futility of
pink, the astonishment of brown. Because she is young and, thus,
still polite, she even nods at the well-intentioned man. Yet the girl
has foretold her future: latitudes and longitudes are delusive
rationales for human logic that never transcends chaos.

I am addicted to what I do not know: hopeless extremity—though
I am uncertain how long I can rely on compassion for consolation.
These are serious days. And I often wonder if you are still uneasy
with smiles. My love, I would wish for you the joy of dying cleanly
but you insist on recreating lakes of ice under pale skies. You have
never known how servitude can become as familiar as oxygen—
that I recognize such somnolence parts the curtain on this
illumination: when I rear out of my own depths, it is to chafe at

eating food earned by someone else, each swallow bequeathing a penetration by something contained within the demeanor of ice.

Once, you said your favorite color is water. That's when I begged you to father my child after I overheard a stranger say, "The love of a parent for a child overwhelms all ties." At the time, I had surrounded myself with perfume and was seeking kindness from several silk scarves unfolded generously before me. I was forced to acquire five when, unexpectedly, I mottled them with my tears. Once more, I engaged in an abuse of guilt, that is, the gnawing of myself that becomes an addiction obviating growth. I try to consider my mistakes with tenderness, only to be relegated to the recompense of nothing; there is not the tiniest redeeming element in how the fabrics manifest glory's different shades: fuschia, lavender, gold, turquoise and celadon. There is not the tiniest redeeming element in my successful foretelling of blustery showers clearing the night for a lemon dawn.

It is time, I shake myself, to visit the museum where Picasso's *Sleeping Nude, 1907*, resides. It is a forthright painting of a woman with no sentimentality. The artist must have looked at the model through a grid—an eye as tender as only detachment can loosen. I wish to belong to a man who sees as Picasso did, to move within the aura of belonging to such a man. *Fit in dominata servitus. In servitude dominatus*: this engagement that surfaces dreams where I am gloriously more than my self. I ache for fictions that would not chasten my days.

Still, I have learned that depression must be precedent to insight—that insight must require humility. Such as when I learned to stop differentiating between "abstract" and "figurative." It was an unexpected revelation from my circling of a column whose colors varied in hue so that I could only comprehend the sculpture through the narrative of time. Lapis lazuli was the color but what I saw were the blue veins on your throat calming themselves an hour after you had muzzled my breasts with hands that behaved as if they resented my flesh. Lapis lazuli was the color and what I saw was solstice.

What is the common denominator of humanity? Yesterday, in the park where trees had stripped into pale limbs, I saw an old couple display affection as if they had never lived through a single world war. I followed the image of clasped hands into a dream whose texture, like rice paper, was so delicate it was difficult to prevent the edges of my vision from shredding. In that dream, I was a child again, taking deep breaths that always deposited into my lungs a sad knowledge: I will manifest my fate of peeling through this lifetime's layers by making decisions that will always require me to adjust. Now, I have passed a certain threshold so that a good day can be defined simply by eating a red apple while walking amidst white snow. I miss New Mexico whose villages I can never attend: where adobe walls are warmed by lanterns of brown paper bags surrounding fat candles aglow.

I am reading *King Lear* and am felled by my instant recognition of how middle-aged indiscretions can sunder the most carefully-planned life. These spasms of human frailty are weak adjustments to death becoming more than a concept. I know this, for when I reach "middle age" I will become addicted to the liberating anonymity that travel confers. Mindanao, Berlin, Melbourne, Amsterdam, Istanbul again and again—you are hours waiting for my flawed counting. Will you share my search for nobility or jeer? Will you weep when you meet me in a tattered gown, clutching a brass crown with cracked jewels of colored glass? Know this first about me: Today I can differentiate between Van Gogh and Gauguin. One understood evil enough not to play with it. One painted morality and showed himself to be a relentlessly good man. Whereas, I cast aside my people, for when I met you I stepped into a parallel universe I had so long inhabited in my imagination. In this universe, my reflection is familiar before I lower my eyes from a joy through which I experience the definition of the word, "replete."

Thus, I did not expect my face today to express the seriousness that is the universal hallmark of motherhood, though I lack the blessing of a single child. My breasts hang with illusion: they have never fed many like Eve's in Piero's painting of *Expulsion from*

Paradise. I woke this morning to the conclusion: I have restricted my life to imagining what it would be like to discover color for the first time. There is no shortcut to such a search—though that search has brought me to a place where I comprehend that tears have no color. Neither does affection. But perseverance does not always suffice, and that I perfect it offers no medals, no ribbons. Inadvertently, I have narrowed my expectations, reducing them to a sort of courtesy. Once, I thought I would never practice diminishment but my life has not exceeded a computer's economic program. I have become my own sculpture: I crawl on floors to see color from different angles but what you see is a block of dark-grey metal that stuns before it swallows light. The block is cold to the touch; its planes offer imperfect squares.

I gaze once more at the sky now hanging low over us all. I am moved to counsel you who have hidden your faces but still listen to my dirge: *Wait. Wait*—delay your mourning. To have given less to my hymns would have birthed a psychic toll much weightier than that stooping my back as I now stand naked and humble before you. *Wait, wait.* A cocoon hangs from a tree like a tender promise, as does an ancient moon afire from the farthest color edging a spectrum. *Wait, wait:* with old age, the grid becomes intuitive. I am optimistic we all may know again that feeling of safety surrounding us before we were born. *Wait, wait.* Defer judgment: Obviate memory.

THE CONTINUANCE OF THE GAZE

— after PROSPECT *by Anne Truitt*

Can you see with such compassion that I might mistake your
lucidity for the high line of a clearing sky, when instead it is the
song of foam cresting a distant wave? Can you pay the price for
risking perception *and* imperceptibility? Can you be surrounded—
sink into, then be uplifted—by the singularity of a color emanating
from a teal painting tiny enough to stand on one hand? I have felt
Michelangelo's slaves surge out of stone. I trust in radiance. Let:
Us.

By moving around an object, toward it or away from it, one
controls its meaning. Is it preferable to narrow the baseline of
one's subjectivity? To limit experience to what is immediately
above and below this wire that links the fragile mind to a heart so
strong it becomes the house of redemption? Can ecstasy
transcend the most momentary meeting with forces that beget
religion—how, in a World War II concentration camp a woman
could have been so cruel to pregnant women by tying their legs
together? I concede no joy in what I have fought so hard to learn:
rupture is Beauty, like the slow walk of childbirth up a spine
frozen in a yearning.

I am trying, you see, to articulate fortitude. Deflections often
guide the course of living. Yet I wish to avoid shrinking away
from exposing my body to my promiscuous mind. How else can
I, with a mere glance, recognize a white bird against a grey sky to
be the same gesture I have been painting for years as a single
brushstroke of turquoise? I treasure the fragmented seconds
when a line of meaning intersects the line of my sight's trajectory.
In those delicate seeds of intersection, I never fail to feel you in
the very air against my cheek—transcending my memory of our
last embrace when your body against mine introduced the limits
of sunlight's expanse. Against all that I have ever learned of

Desire—against everything that is a natural instinct to me—I foretold the permanence of absence against my lonely breasts.

How dangerous: the sky! Without a horizon, the sky manifests a physical infinity. I wish to bear this lack of limits, but the eye clamors against the reverse of claustrophobia. The eye consistently searches for a perch so that one can see with context. I make do with the sheen of stones and rivers within sunlit days— sunshine so brilliant I come to see a lapis lazuli color as indomitable. I fear so many things, after all, from the ripening of a mango to the scalpel hovering over my father's heart to feeling the fragility of your existence with the unyielding onset of my amnesia. How to reconcile with my childish refusal to shade my eyes when fate is a form of will: I attract what I fear? These are among the many words, you see, that I have uttered, only to pray they become like raindrops into the lake of a mischievous god's forgetfulness. Of course, I (perversity defining me as much as any other concept) must now tempt fate by publicly conceding: I also fear the possibility of a broken blood vessel dotting the eye an unforgiving scarlet.

Still, I must not forego the delight of neutrality. How the totality of white allows a canvas to reveal the chaos of color, the pulse of a shade, the flux of meaning. Too often, I am histrionic, thereby creating my own chains. I know the imperatives of my desire and pain are colored green, like the glimmer of Antarctic berg ice. Green ice is thought to have been exposed by the shear of mountain glaciers. Somehow, the ice survives intact and rides out into the South Atlantic Ocean—a broken rib of emerald from a maternal continent! Still, I must not forego the wisdom of neutrality, even if the best I can muster is jade: still green, but with an unperturbed face.

I sense that I will end this day, this poem, with the inability to distinguish between a human scream and a high wind. *Duende*— it exposes with insistence just a half-breath away from savagery. I could not have predicted the price of masterfully cultivating what is within me: I am addicted to Art that arises as it wills from vacuums that laugh at my attempts to measure them. Though I treasure fragile violets that dare to bloom ahead of spring, this is a sentence of diversion. *Duende*, Garcia Lorca reminds, is two-faced to enable death and geometry to infiltrate each other's worlds. Now, I greet each day as an exposed nerve. Oh, sometimes, I wish merely to be pale. That is not all: too often, I finally surface from verdant depths to see a sky so lurid it is nonreverberative.

Thus, artists end in their beginnings: the memory of memories. Water evaporates into air: we end with knowing failure: the invaluable predicate of all honest compassion. I am struck by how often I leave others with mere marks that evoke the pawing of animals that hunt. Through this path, I have learned how yellow can look decidedly determined. I believe I now realize I prefer psychological insecurity—yes, even that dark path where I fell to my knees and still (oh still!) you showed no pity. The capacity for recognizing the colors of perseverance matters, you see. Color is also a narrative—even when aesthetically displeasing to the eye. Yet, always, worthy is the price. I *shall* retain the capacity to feel you in the breeze lifting my hair from the palpable nape of my neck. Always, worthy is the price: Yes!

SELECTED NOTES TO POEMS

ABANDONING MISERY
The first stanza's reference to Burkina Faso was inspired by the lines, "and always there is someone in Burkina Faso/ who cannot sleep" in "Lyrics from a Dead Language" by Eric Gamalinda (EG). The second stanza's first poet refers to a statement by Barbara Guest in a Lannan Literary Video; the second poet refers to a statement by Anais Nin in *Nearer The Moon* (Harcourt Brace. & Co., 1996); and the third poet refers to a conversation with EG. A "datsan" is a Buddhist colony; the poem refers to the author's trip to the Igolvinsk datsan in Siberia in April 1996. The third stanza references Homer's *Odyssey*.

AMBER
The first stanza's quote is from the gospel of Saint Paul. The third stanza's reference to the Irish poet relates to Eavan Boland who wrote "Letter To A Young Woman Poet" (*American Poetry Review*, May/June 1997), in which she suggests: "*the past needs us.* That very past in poetry which simplified us . . . now needs us to change it. . . .Therefore we need to change the past. Not by intellectualizing it. But by eroticizing it. . . . a template of poetic authority can actually be changed, altered, radicalized by those very aspects of humanity which are excluded from it . . ."

THE BEGINNING
The referenced oil portrait was inspired by "Robin" by Gregory Gillespie.

COROLLA
The first draft of the poem was "collaged" from fragments of fiction and poetry written by over fifty writers featured in *BABAYLAN: An Anthology of Filipina and Filipina American Writers* (Aunt Lute Press, 2000).

INSOMNIA'S LULLABYE
Pusod = navel
Balut = a delicacy of boiled duck embryo egg
Sinigang = soup of fish and tamarind
Longanisa = sausage

THE INVESTMENT BANKER
The poem was inspired by a September 13, 1996 reading by Mei-mei Berssenbrugge at the Asian American Writers Workshop which was attended by several investment bankers from Union Bank of Switzerland,

Merrill Lynch and Morgan Stanley. During the 1980s and 1990s, the author was an international project finance banker.

RESPECT
The second stanza's phrase, "looking between raindrops," references "The Untroubled Mind" by Agnes Martin wherein she says, "Don't look at the stars. . . . Look between the rain. The drops are insular." A "fado" is a plaintive Portuguese folk song.

RETURNING THE BORROWED TONGUE
Jaime Jacinto's poem, ": Looking for Buddha" was published in the anthology, *Breaking Silence* (ed. Joseph Bruchac, The Greenfield Review Press, 1983), hence its reference in the fourth stanza.

THE SOULFUL UNIVERSE
The second and fourth stanza quotes are from an article about Lee Smolin titled "The Cosmos According to Darwin" by Dennis Overbye (*The New York Times Magazine*, July 13, 1997).

ACKNOWLEDGEMENTS

I am grateful to the Fundacion Valparaiso (Spain), MacDowell Colony, Ucross Foundation, Villa Montalvo, and Virginia Center For The Creative Arts where I wrote poems for this collection. *Salamat* to Anvil Publishing (Manila), the Asian American Writers Workshop (New York), Bindlestiff Studios (San Francisco), Giraffe Books (Quezon City), Marsh Hawk Press (New York), Pusod Center (Berkeley) and Flips Listserve (Cyberspace).

Some of these poems (or earlier versions) first appeared in *Asian Pacific American Journal; BagongPinay; Coracle; Crab Orchard Review; Ekphrasis; The Evening Paper; Fuel; Interlope; Intersection Magazine; Kimera; Luna; OurOwnVoice; Pen & Ink; Outlet; phati'tude; Readme; Reasonable Earthquakes; RIO: A Journal of the Arts; Rockhurst Review; Sidereality: A Journal of Speculative & Experimental Poetry; SugarMule; Tinfish; Tamafhyr Mountain Poetry;* and *xStream.* Some poems were featured in the anthologies: *Technologies of Measure: A Celebration of Bay Area Women Writers* (Eds. Rena Rosenwasser, Elizabeth Treadwell, Kate Colby and Nikki Thompson, organized by Small Press Traffic, Kelsey St. Press and Yerba Buena Center for the Arts, San Francisco, 2002); *Short Fuse: A Global Anthology of New Fusion Poetry* (Eds. Todd Swift and Philip Norton, Ratapallax Press, New York, 2002); *Eros Pinoy: An Anthology of Contemporary Erotica in Philippine Art and Poetry* (Eds. Virgilio Aviado, Ben Cabrera and Alfred A. Yuson, Anvil, Manila, 2001); *Babaylan: An Anthology of Filipina and Filipina-American Writers* (Ed. Nick Carbo, Aunt Lute Press, San Francisco, 2000); *The Nuyorasian Anthology* (Ed. Bino A. Realuyo, Asian American Writers Workshop, New York, 1999); *FIL-AM* (Eds. Alfred Yuson and Eric Gamalinda, PubliCo, Inc., Manila, 1999); and *Poetry Nation: The North American Anthology of Fusion Poetry* (Eds. Regie Cabico and Todd Swift, Vehicule Press, Montreal, Quebec, 1998). Some poems were recorded in the CD *The Empty Flagpole* (Producer Theo Gonzalves, Jeepney Dash Productions, San Francisco, 2000). "MUSE POEM" was inspired by Robert Roth's print entitled "Mask Implosion" and written for *When Butterflies Speak,* a 1998 collaboration between poets/writers and visual artists sponsored by the Skylight Gallery of Brooklyn, New York (curator: Ted Lawton).

For love, friendship and encouragement during the formation of this manuscript, *Agyamanac unay* to the poets Carlos Angeles, Jose Ayala,

Michelle Bautista, Mei-mei Berssenbrugge, Luis Cabalquinto, Nick Carbo, Oliver de la Paz, Ruel S. de Vera, Patricia Dienstfrey, Denise Duhamel, Thomas Fink, Sesshu Foster, Luis Francia, Forrest Gander, Eric Gamalinda, Eugene Gloria, Reme Grefalda, Ken Gurney, Kimiko Hahn, Paolo Javier, Andrew Joron, Summi Kaipa, Molly McQuade, Michelle Murphy, Rene Navarro, Ishle Park, Jukka Pekka-Kervinen, Bino A. Realuyo, Barbara Jane Reyes, Rena Rosenwasser, Nadine Sarreal, Susan Schultz, Barry Schwabsky, Purvi Shah, Gary Sullivan, Arthur Sze, Elizabeth Treadwell, John Yau, and Alfred Yuson. And to writers and scholars who aided my thoughts on decolonized poetics: E. San Juan, Leny M. Strobel, Theo Gonzalves and M. Evelina Galang. For his Faith: Thomas Pollock. *Dios Ti Agngina.*

EILEEN R. TABIOS majored in political science at Barnard College and received an M.B.A. in economics and international business from New York University's Graduate School of Business. She has released a poetry CD and written, edited or co-edited nine books of poetry, fiction and essays since 1996 when she traded in a finance career for poetry. Her awards include the Philippines' Manila Critics Circle National Book Award for Poetry, the Potrero Nuevo Fund Prize, the PEN/Oakland Josephine Miles National Literary Award, a Witter Bynner Poetry Grant and a PEN Open Book Award. Much of her creative writing are inspired by the visual arts. In 2001, she began to explore ways to create poems with physical bodies and multidimensional spaces. The results include mixed-media sculptures, drawings, installations, a performance wedding ceremony "happening" and collaborations with artists from a variety of disciplines; the works form her "Poems Form/From The Six Directions" project which has been exhibited at various Bay Area (California) locations. She is the founder of Meritage Press, a multidisciplinary literary and arts publisher based in St. Helena, CA where, as a budding grape farmer, she is arduously researching the poetry of wine.